GIRL IN THE BELGIAN RESISTANCE

GIRL IN THE BELGIAN RESISTANCE

A WAKEFUL EYE IN THE UNDERGROUND

FERNANDE K. DAVIS

Second Edition with
Foreword by Hanna Diamond

Beach Lloyd
PUBLISHERS
LLC
WAYNE, PENNSYLVANIA

Beach Lloyd Publishers, September 2008
Copyright © 2008 by Fernande Davis
Second Edition
First Edition ISBN 978-0-9792778-7-0 published July 2008

* * * * *

Library of Congress Cataloging-in-Publication Data

Davis, Fernande.
  Girl in the Belgian resistance : a wakeful eye in the underground / Fernande Davis. -- 2nd ed. / with foreword by Hanna Diamond.
      p. cm.
  Includes bibliographical references.
  ISBN 978-0-9792778-9-4 (alk. paper)
  1. Davis, Fernande. 2. World War, 1939-1945--Underground movements--Belgium. 3. World War, 1939-1945--Personal narratives, Belgian. 4. Belgium--History--German occupation, 1940-1945. 5. Teenage girls--Belgium--Biography. I. Title.

  D802.B4D28 2008b
  940.53'493092--dc22
  [B]

                          2008039832

Book design by Joanne S. Silver.
Technical direction by Ronald Silver.
Illustrations are the author's personal photographs, unless
    otherwise credited.
Cover by David Moore.
Cover image by Sharon Bagatta: Fernande evacuating from
    Andenne.   .

This Memoir is dedicated

To my dear parents,
who taught me about
faith, love and family

To my beloved Bill,
who was my hero,
my liberator and my husband

To my children, Patricia and Bill Jr.,
my grand-children Laura, Liam,
Sean, Saralynne and Erica,
and to my great-grand-daughter Elizabeth

So they will know the tapestry
of Grammy's young life.

Contents

Foreword   *xi*
Acknowledgments   *xv*
Introduction   *xvii*

PART ONE: BEFORE THE WAR—1939
    01 Safe Haven   *1*
    02 Leaving Montzen for Andenne   *7*
    03 Andenne   *11*

PART TWO: EVACUATION & OCCUPATION—1940
    04 Bicycles and Barnyards   *15*
    05 German Overtake   *19*
    06 Deadly Pastures   *25*
    07 Return to Andenne   *29*
    08 Home to Montzen   *31*
    09 Church Bells to Bullets   *35*
    10 Uncle Alphonse   *37*

PART THREE: DRAFTED—the First Leap of Faith—1942
    11 Jump, Drop, and Roll   *43*
    12 The Long Road to Hiding   *47*

PART FOUR: LIÈGE & THE RESISTANCE—1942–1944
    13 Liège at Last   *51*
    14 Dangerous Rescue   *57*
    15 False IDs to Banneux   *65*
    16 Raid on Liège   *71*
    17 First Communion at Saint Bartholomew's   *77*
    18 My Family at Home during the War   *83*
    19 Bombardment of Montzen Gare   *87*
    20 Digging Out   *91*
    21 My Years in the Underground   *97*

PART FIVE: THE LIBERATION—1945
    22 Return to Montzen   *103*
    23 The Miracle of the Piano   *107*
    24 Bill and Me   *111*
    25 Bill in Germany   *117*
    26 Promises to Keep   *121*

Epilogue   *127*
Discussion Questions
        General   *131*   Content-Directed   *132*
References Used   *137*
Further Study: Bibliography, Videography, Webography   *137*

Illustrations

Map of Belgium.   *xvi*

The church in Montzen, a central part of village life.   *3*

Montzen Town Square and the pharmacy (center).   *3*

Montzen Elementary School.   *4*

The road to Montzen Gare.   *4*

The Keufgens homestead, our safe haven before the war. I was the first child born there. (Post-war repair shows white streaks on the façade.)   *5*

The Keufgens family in the garden behind our home—ca. 1937. From left: Joseph, « Jeanon », Marie, Théo, Berthe, Cécile, Fernande, Hubert, Maman, Papa.   *5*

The villa in Andenne.   *9*

Papa and Uncle Hubert in Verdun during World War I.   *12*

Civilian exodus. Belgians fleeing to France.   *18*

Entrance to a Belgian farm similar to that in Beauvais.   *19*

The farm in Beauvais (likeness)—the homestead wing.   *20*

Exit from the courtyard to the bunker (likeness).   *21*

The cement foundation, all that remains of Uncle Alphonse and Tante Martine's house. On the right, the old railroad crossing.   *38*

The viaduct connecting Belgium to Aachen, Germany. Above, far left: the spot where I jumped off the train. Bottom: the viaduct after the war, blown up by the Germans.   *44*

Lush Belgian farmland.   *49*

Uncle Hubert, 1914–1918. Picture given to me with his note on the back: "Have courage."   *53*

Uncle Hubert's rectory. On the top floor, near the third window on the left, we used to crawl out of the skylight and hide on the roof when the Germans came for inspection.   *54*

The false identification card, actually a false work card [Arbeitskarte]. The Germans treated it as identification, work for the war effort being their primary interest.   *55*

The farm, modernized today, where I fetched Josh (X above the door).   *57*

Cow in the meadow (likeness).   *60*

The area that Josh/Pierre and I traveled to reach Liege.   *61*

Sanatorium run by Franciscan nuns to care for children with tuberculosis. After the war, the building was enlarged, named L'Hospitalité, and became a welcome place for pilgrims to Banneux. (story in chapter 15).   *64*

The shrine of Banneux.   *66*

The Church of Saint Bartholomew.   *77*

Father Jean Arnolds.   *82*

Destruction of Montzen Gare (1).   *89*

Destruction of Montzen Gare (2) and a bomb crater.   *90*

Château Belderbusch (XVIth century) before the bombings.   *93*

Château Belderbusch after the bombardments.   *93*

Clandestine letter of warning to Resistance workers (translation, p. 99).   *98*

Translation of letter of warning, hand delivered to me in July 1944, only days before the arrival of Americans in Liège.   *99*

Fernande on the rue du Fer. The baby grand piano was lifted over this balcony under a rainstorm of V1 and V2 bombs.   *110*

Fernande in Bill's helmet.   *112*

The photo of Fernande that Bill took with him to the front.   *114*

Fernande and Bill in the park in Liège, Belgium—1945.   *116*

Wedding photo. Fernande and Bill—October 27, 1949.   *126*

Papa at age 83.   *127*

This beautiful sunny morning

I ride down our country road.

Chirping birds announce the new day

Morning Glories blossom

and lilacs perfume the air.

My heavy bicycle gently sways,

My skirt and my blue hat flap in the wind.

All seems lovely,

but NOTHING is the same!

Foreword
Hanna Diamond, PhD

This moving account tells the story of Fernande Davis, who was fifteen in 1940, the third child of a large family of eight children. Her narrative is particularly interesting to the historian for what we learn about this area of Belgium during the war. It was not just occupied by the Germans, but annexed by the Reich, rendering it a part of Germany from May 1940 until September 1944, when these territories were liberated by American troops. It is rare to find accounts of everyday life and resistance in this part of Belgium where the intense German presence made any resistance involvement extremely dangerous.

Fernande's family lived in the small village of Montzen Gare, a cross-border area situated close to the German/Dutch border and just twenty kilometers from Aachen in Germany, which could be seen on a good day. This community was strongly marked by its experiences of the previous war when the Germans had occupied Belgium for four years. Its position so close to the frontier meant that the inhabitants had a strong sense of impending war well before the actual German invasion. A First World War veteran, Fernande's astute father fully expected invasion and planned carefully for it. He laid extensive plans in advance and arranged for his teenage daughter to be placed as a lady's help in Andenne, a small town away from the German frontier and outside the annexed territories. His main concern was to protect her from potential deportation to work in Germany. His fears were well founded when soon after annexation, young people over fourteen from the area were drafted to Germany to work for them. It took some time for the Germans to track Fernande down, but they did finally catch up with her in 1942. Fernande refused to contemplate following a draft order to work in an ammunition factory in Danzig and jumped from the train which was due to take her there, and made her way to her uncle's home in Liège. From then onwards she was based there, in hiding, and started a clandestine life.

Her accounts of her work passing refugees across the border established by the Germans between occupied and annexed territory and her work as a courier are gripping and real. If she had been caught she would certainly have been deported to a concentration camp. There is no doubt that this young woman was aware of the seriousness of the risks she ran, not just for her own sake, but she also carried the ever-present fear that her arrest would jeopardise the work of other members of her father's family as well as those who were working alongside them. Her position as a German speaker, having been brought up in this cross-border region, meant that she could convincingly pass herself off as a German native, and she used this successfully on a number of occasions to escape round-ups and dupe German patrols and guards. We can only admire the remarkable courage and bravery of this sixteen-year-old to have been able to pull this off.

Religion was clearly an important part of Fernande's resistance commitment, and most of her activities were centered around the work of her Uncle Hubert, a Catholic priest. Her stories illuminate the ways in which this group of Catholics risked everything to hide Jews and help them escape occupied territory. Interestingly, the privacy of the confessional was subverted to become an invaluable means of communication between resisters. None of them could ever relax. They always slept half dressed in case they had to flee an unexpected police patrol.

Fernande's account of her family's experiences provides a moving snapshot of everyday life in these annexed territories. While "no one lived a normal life," populations developed strategies of survival which often served them well. She describes "the small gestures of rebuttal, refusal and rejection" which marked the relationships between locals and the Germans. Remarkably, this German-speaking community appears to have asserted itself quite successfully and even managed to gain concessions from their Occupiers on occasion. This may suggest that they were treated somewhat differently from the populations of other occupied areas.

When Montzen was finally liberated in 1944, Fernande fell in love with an American soldier who remained in Liège for four months. Her devout father had to fight his reluctance to see her leave the family once again and strike out for a new existence across the Atlantic.

Where historical interest has tended to focus on more formal networks of escape routes and intelligence gathering, this compelling testimony offers us invaluable insights into a more spontaneous but equally important form of Belgian resistance. The value of this kind of memoir is that it provides us with information about the life of communities and individuals at this traumatic time. Fernande Davis's story shows us how the Resistance operated, for those brave enough to take such risks, as an ongoing daily involvement.

Hanna Diamond is Senior Lecturer in French History and European Studies at the University of Bath, UK. She is author of Women and the Second World War in France 1939–48: choices and constraints *(1999, Longman) and* Fleeing Hitler: France 1940 *(2007, Oxford University Press).*

Preface

I have written this Memoir of my two and a half years in the Belgian Resistance at the request of my family and colleagues at Germantown Academy.

After World War II, I came to the United States in 1949, was married, had two children and returned to college to finish my education.

I taught French for twenty-two years, four of them at Gwynedd Mercy Academy and College, and eighteen at Germantown Academy.

I was invited by the late Mister Biggs, Assistant Headmaster at the Academy at the time, to speak to his history class, and I became keenly aware that people knew much about the Holocaust, but little about the dangerous work of the Resistance. The students demonstrated a real interest in what happened to this sixteen-year-old girl during the war.

Today, the Academy often invites me to return, and I am also pleased to honor requests of our former French teacher, Madame Briane Horner, to speak in several schools in Connecticut where she has taught.

My profound gratitude goes to the following people for their assistance during the creation of this memoir: to Emily Wagner for her help, love and ongoing support in the writing of "my story for the children," and for introducing me to Ron and Joanne Silver, making this publication possible.

To my dear friend Briane Horner for originally insisting that my experiences be recorded, and to Briane and her husband Steve for offering the peace and tranquility of their lakeshore home in Maine, and their encouragement in getting started. Also, to Elaine Crump for whisking me off to her peaceful Ocean City dwelling when I needed calm without interruptions.

A warm thank goes to my family, especially to Barbara Parsons Davis and her husband William

Davis for their guidance, and the countless hours spent teaching me the ways of the computer, and to daughter Patricia and husband William for their steadfast vote of confidence. Thank you also for the support of my friends here in the U.S., and family in Belgium. I am most grateful for interviews granted by Mr. and Mrs. Vercheval of Jalhay, Belgium and Mr. and Mrs. Jean-Pierre Gillot of Seilles, Belgium. Thank you to my brother, Father Hubert Keufgens, who procured permission for reproducing the village post-cards from Monsieur L. Langohr of Montzen, and went *sur place* to photograph the countryside and the remains of Uncle Alphonse's house.

I will forever feel deeply indebted to Ginny Hunter, our teacher of Creative Writing at Foulkeways, for her enthusiasm and willingness to share insights and reflections, and for the innumerable hours she spent proofreading the manuscript. Without her support and confidence, this book could not have been written. To my classmates in Ginny's 2007 class, "merci" for your support and all the fun.

Last but not least, to the people of Germantown Academy for their work and support of this project—in particular to Donna Merow for her proofreading of the manuscript and to Dainis Roman for his patience and practical help with videotaping. To one and all at Germantown Academy, my sincerest appreciation.

For our children, this is my story!

* * * * *

.

Introduction

In 1922, my parents built their eight-bedroom dream house, an impressive three-story brick home in Montzen Gare [Montzen Station], a small village in Belgium with a population of 2,700, near the border of Germany and Holland.

We were surrounded by a few houses and lovely farmland. Our favorite baker was across the street. Our paternal grandfather's farm was about 500 meters up the road; the meadow where his cows grazed ended across the street from our house. The left side of our house was flanked by a piece of land the size of a small football field leading up to the immense railroad yard of Montzen Station. A tiny part of the station was devoted to passenger trains that would take workers, shoppers and students to the city of Verviers, or to the high school in Visé. Looking eastward toward Germany from the front of our house, we could imagine the enemy's borders that lay a short distance from our village.

The fear of another war still loomed over the area since Germany's invasion of Belgium in 1914 and occupation of the country for four long years. During that time our little railroad changed drastically. Germany began building a gigantic viaduct connecting Aachen, Germany to Visé, Belgium. Thousands of Russian prisoners were forced into labor. Many had no experience in construction or were not physically able to do hard and dangerous work, and died in the process.

Belgium completed the viaduct after World War I ended. While Germany had left so much of our country in ruins, one could look at the famous viaduct of Moresnet as an exception to the carnage. It was recognized as a true *chef d'œuvre* [masterpiece].

Traffic at Montzen Gare gradually increased. More rails were needed for the importing and exporting of merchandise. Trains would stop in Montzen to pass customs and inspection. The yard also had a huge depot where trains and locomotives came in for repair. By 1940, 147 parallel rails lay in this huge railyard to accommodate the traffic.

Little did we know that by 1940 our quiet little Montzen Gare had become strategic to Hitler's war effort. Our viaduct gave him a direct line to Visé, Hasselt, and on up to the port of Antwerp, which would facilitate his plan to reach and overtake England. Throughout the war, huge trainloads of stolen goods from France and Belgium came through Montzen and rolled over the viaduct to Germany.

During the war, Germany annexed territory east of the dotted line; what was formerly Belgium became Germany, until the Liberation.

01 **Safe Haven**

A small country village with a lush green square, a water fountain and a well-built kiosk in the center, where the band would play and entertain the villagers on all major occasions. The church, the school, the town hall, the burgomaster's home, the only pharmacy in town, one or two small stores to buy candy, pencils or postcards, and private dwellings to complete the perimeter of the square. That was Montzen Village. We walked to it every day from our home in Montzen Gare, and it encompassed an integral part of our young lives.

Each morning, my sister Mary and I would wake up to the sounds of the farm help calling the animals in for milking. If the weather was nice, we would hang out the bedroom window and laugh at this little man racing down the field, swinging his long whip and yelling at the top of his voice to bring the cows into the barn. One of them would never obey! It had a mind of its own and would always run in the opposite direction or behind the caller, making him turn back on his heels and run like a fool. Mary and I would scream and laugh so hard we'd wake up the rest of the house.

Sometimes, after the cows were in the barn, Maman would ask if anyone wanted to go and pick fresh mushrooms in that field.

We would climb over the fence across the street, discard our wooden shoes near the hedge, and do our mushroom search barefooted. We believed that the morning dew on our bare feet was good for our health, but at six in the morning the grass was cold and wet, a rude awakening! We had fun going barefoot, searching for the nice-looking white heads that were there peeking out through the wet, green grass. My brother Joseph and I were always in competition as to who could fill our basket first. These early morning adventures were always followed by a delicious pan of hot sautéed mushrooms with homemade bread before heading out to church or to school.

We were a close family and, as children, we lived a sheltered and carefree life with little to worry about. Papa, on the other hand, was seriously following the news. He read French and German newspapers and listened intently to reports on the radio about Hitler's ambitions and aggressions through Europe. He felt that Hitler's invasion of Belgium was imminent. The location of our village of Montzen, only a few kilometers from the German border, heightened his anxiety. Papa had fought the Germans in World War I, and was wounded and gassed in Verdun. His fear of another war was well-justified; he would have to think of ways to protect his teenage children and his family.

Joseph, my oldest brother, seemed secure in his work for the telephone company. The Germans would need his service. The chances of drafting him looked remote.

My oldest sister, Bertha, was needed in the household and in our family country store. She was also a seamstress and helped my parents financially by sewing for people in the village. Papa felt that the Germans would accept her employment as a bona fide occupation. She would stay home.

At fifteen, I was the third child of the family. Three girls and two boys came after me. With the threat of Hitler's approach, I was considered vulnerable. Papa decided that I would have to be placed somewhere in the central part of Belgium, away from the border.

A wartime friend of his, who lived with his sister in a lovely chalet in Andenne, would be happy to have me. He was a captain in the reserves and was called back to duty, like every able-bodied male between the age of twenty-five and fifty. Papa was exempt. He was no longer classified as "able-bodied"—the first war had seen to that! The captain's sister, Mademoiselle Madeleine, was left alone in her house and would need assistance. I would be well remunerated and could help ease the financial burden of my family.

The Church in Montzen, a central part of village life.

Foto Lander Eupen (B)

Montzen Town Square and the pharmacy (center).

Foto Lander Eupen (B)

Montzen Elementary School.

Foto Lander Eupen (B)

The Road to Montzen Gare.

Foto Lander Eupen (B)

The Keufgens homestead, our safe haven before the war. I was the first child born there. (Post-war repair shows white streaks on the façade.)

The Keufgens family in the garden behind our home—ca. 1937. From left: Joseph, « Jeanon », Marie, Théo, Berthe, Cécile, Fernande, Hubert, Maman, Papa.

02 **Leaving Montzen for Andenne**

Reluctantly, but with wonder and excitement at going by myself to the unknown, I bid my family good-bye, crossed the field adjacent to our house, and reached the little station of Montzen Gare, where I took the local train to Verviers. From there I would catch a connecting train to Andenne, in the central part of Belgium. It was January 1940.

As the train slowly pulled out of the station, I glanced out the window and was shocked at the sight of my sister Mary, running on the platform next to the train. She was still wearing her apron, had no coat on, and was frantically waving a pair of shoes while screaming my name, to get my attention. I jumped up from my seat, pulled down my window panel and grabbed my black-heeled Sunday shoes from her outstretched arm. I had, as usual, forgotten some of my belongings and, most importantly, the only pair of shoes I had to go to church on Sunday! What a scene I created!

With both arms stretched out of the window, I frantically sent her kisses, which did not alleviate my embarrassment or the pain I felt for poor Mary standing there, red-faced and exhausted. I wanted to scream how much I loved her, but train schedules do not allow for long, sentimental good-byes. Mary disappeared slowly into the distance. I slid back into my seat and wiped away tears of remorse and sadness at leaving my dearest sister and family.

The ride south and beyond the city of Liège was intriguing. I had never been this far from home. I was discovering a new world with very different scenery. The industrial parts of Belgium with their factories, warehouses and smokestacks lacked the human aspects of life that I loved. Before I had time to lament, the signs were announcing our arrival in Andenne.

The captain was waiting for me at the station. He was a tall, good-looking officer in full dress uniform.

His military rank was written all over his face. He was both determined and deliberate as he shook my hand and swung my meager luggage into the back seat of his car. With a commanding tone he said, "Come, Fernande. We'll take a short ride to Mademoiselle, and I will be off to rejoin my unit."

Intimidated, I quickly sat next to my host in total obedience. I felt as though I was being inducted into the army. *What would be his next command? Should I be clicking my heels and saluting?* Within minutes he took off like a race car driver. I was breathless. I never saw the ground pass by my window this fast. I silently started to recite a prayer—an act of contrition that we Catholics recite after confessing our sins—just in case I should die.

In a flash, the car slowed down and we rolled into a street lined with trees. A long building that looked like stables was on the right and a lovely villa was directly opposite on the left. We had arrived! The captain flung open my car door with the same gusto he had demonstrated with his driving.

It's hard to forget the feeling of relief when I first set eyes on the beautiful lady standing on the side porch of this cozy-looking villa. She greeted us, hugged her brother *au revoir,* and invited me in. Mademoiselle seemed to be the opposite of her brother. "Come," said she, "do not be afraid of Monsieur Jean. He is an exuberant man, but kind."

She was a tall and trim lady of, perhaps, my mother's age. She had a kind smile, a soft voice, and gorgeous blond hair piled on the top of her head, held in place by an unusual silver comb. I was ushered into the salon with a lovely marble fireplace. Mademoiselle had prepared a cup of hot chocolate and some *biscottes* for us, and we chatted for a long, long time.

She informed me that my duties would be to keep her company and to help with household chores and animal care. Then she showed me the rest of the house, including my room, and invited me to come down and have supper with her as soon as I had unpacked the few things I had brought.

I went to bed that night feeling that I liked my new home with Mademoiselle Madeleine.

The villa in Andenne.

03 **Andenne**

Life in Andenne was quiet and uneventful for a few months. My days were filled with chores, some of which I had never done before. If Mademoiselle's brother, Monsieur Jean, was home for a brief time, he would want a lot of attention and his breakfast served in bed. His sister would always make him something special with a good cup of coffee, but I was to take the tray up the narrow stairs to his room—without spilling the coffee into the saucer. I was uncomfortable going into this strange man's bedroom and would drop the tray onto his nightstand and run back down before he had a chance to ask me to do anything else for him.

Mademoiselle did the cooking, but it was up to me to get the vegetables cleaned and ready for the *pot-au-feu* [stew]. There was nobody to talk to except Mademoiselle, and she was a quiet, introverted person who did not converse easily. She adored her brother, but he was absent most of the time. My days consisted of doing chores, like cleaning the house or polishing the silver. It was so boring I would often sing, like my own mother used to in the early morning. I was happy when it was time to go to the stable to feed the chickens and collect their fresh eggs, even when they were still sitting on their nests and would cluck angrily at me. Feeding the pigs was fun, but I never got used to cleaning their sties. It was an onerous job that had to be done regardless of my dislike.

By sunup their German shepherd could hardly wait to come across the street to the house for the day. Sometimes Mademoiselle would come to help me clean the stables and put clean hay on the floors, but when I had to do it alone, I would talk to the animals, giving them names as though they were people. To my amazement, there was one chicken who would always answer and cackle back at me.

I had no days off and would be allowed off the property only to go with one of their bicycles to the farm for milk, or to the store for groceries. The house, the animals and the garden kept me busy and out of trouble, but I was lonely. The Sunday outings to church and to visit Mademoiselle's friend Margot in the adjacent village did nothing for me.

There was no phone and no way of communicating with my family. Visits home to see my siblings were scheduled by Papa and were limited to once every few weeks. I spent many nights reading or simply gazing out the window, thinking of them and wishing they were closer to us.

I can't remember exactly how long I was in Andenne before the war started. Perhaps five months. A lonely time it was!

During the winter months, I worried about Papa. He had been gassed during World War I, and the injuries inflicted at the battle of Verdun left him with a slight limp. As he advanced in years, he often became very ill during the cold weather, and he suffered increasingly from pneumonia.

Papa and Uncle Hubert in Verdun during World War I.

I can remember a few episodes when his brother-priest, our Uncle Hubert, was called to the house. Every time this happened, Papa's doctor would tell Maman that there was very little hope for survival. We children would be called to the bedside to kneel all around the bed while Uncle Hubert led us in prayers.

During one very bad spell, before antibiotics were widely available, Papa's fever was so elevated that he became delirious. He had not spoken for days. We were all kneeling at his bedside, loudly praying the rosary, waiting for what we thought might be the end, while Father Hubert administered the sacrament of the dying.

As we pleaded with God not to take our dear Papa away, he opened his eyes and murmured, *"Ça va,"* (assuring us that he was alright). Even at that tender age, I was convinced that miracles could happen, because Papa always recovered.

By the next morning, things would look normal. Papa would be moving around and looking alive. Maman would be in the kitchen making breakfast, before sending us to church and to school. Painful moments such as these made an indelible print on my mind. I often worried about Papa while I was alone in Andenne.

My reminiscing and boredom soon came to an end as I watched and listened to neighbors gathering on the streets. People were nervous and fearful. Talk of war was everywhere. Would there be another war? Would Germany invade us again? Would our army be able to stop them? These fears were expressed by everyone I met on the street.

Then came that fateful day of May 10, 1940.

Sirens screamed through the dawn of our peaceful Andenne. We ran out into the garden and street to stare up at the sky. We saw what we thought was a squadron of the Belgian Air Force approaching, only to be horrorstruck at the sight of swastikas on the tails of the planes. Total panic set in as we ran to the radio to find that, yes, *"les Boches"* (the derogatory word used to describe the German invaders) had invaded Belgium once more. The radio frantically announced the retreat of our Belgian forces and the German occupation of that border zone.

IT WAS WAR!

My family's home was located just a short distance from Aachen, Germany. The invaders had conquered all border towns and were rapidly advancing into Belgium. I was stranded—no longer able to go home. If I tried to return home, I would be running right into the lion's mouth and that would have been tantamount to suicide.

All I could think about were my parents and brothers and sisters. *Could they have survived such an assault? When would I see them again? Was there any way to help them? What could we do?*

* * * * *

04 **Bicycles and Barnyards**

The memory of the cruelty and violence of the Germans during World War I triggered strong feelings throughout Belgium. People were filled with anger and indignation but, above all, fear. Most citizens of Andenne saw only one option: evacuate! Run toward France and hope that the Belgian army, helped by English and French troops, would stop the invasion. People were willing to leave all possessions behind, to run for their lives. Little did they imagine how powerful and well-prepared Hitler's army was.

Mademoiselle and I hurriedly grabbed one small leather suitcase each, to carry necessities for a few days. We both tried to conceal some of our most precious possessions. Madeleine wrapped her beautiful jewels in her fine undergarments, but there was no time to think of important papers or anything else. We left everything behind in the hope that we would find it on our return.

Each piece of luggage must have weighed thirty pounds. A family car was a rare item to possess in that little town, and Mademoiselle did not have one. Her brother had taken his precious sports car when he left to rejoin his army unit. We each had a bicycle at our disposal.

Mademoiselle was a dainty lady and looked totally incapable of maneuvering a bicycle with a heavy suitcase strapped on it. She could not move the bike, let alone ride it up and down the hills of the surrounding Ardennes. It was decided that I would be the carrier of luggage. One was tied onto the luggage rack in front, secured by leather straps around the handle bars, and the second, tied onto the luggage rack in back, gave me enough equilibrium to ride.

My most cherished item was a gift from Maman for Easter, a beautiful blue summer hat with a large brim that floated in the wind. Maman had been a hatmaker by profession before she was married. She would make sure that every few years her girls got a new hat for Easter.

With me coiffed in my lovely *chapeau*, we set out to join the thousands of evacuees on the road south to France. I was amazed at the balance I was able to maintain on my loaded bike and the speed I would attain going downhill. It was almost fun but challenging. I would reach a dangerous speed going downhill and pedal hard to make it halfway up the next hill.

By now the Belgian and French armies were marching on these same roads, going in the opposite direction. They were heading north to confront the Germans at the front line, hoping to halt the invaders. With their machine guns, tanks and trucks, they commandeered the roads.

Thousands of families with horses and wagons, even wheelbarrows, were fleeing. They were stacked with bundles of clothes, pillows, mattresses, cooking utensils and food, leaving space only for the elderly and a few small children to ride. Bicycles and motorcycles too, had meager possessions strapped on, as all headed for safety into France. An unimaginable tableau! We were a mass of humanity bound by the same fear and panic.

Little food was available because people could take only what they could carry. Water was not always safe to drink. Lodging was not to be found, sleeping was *à la belle étoile,* "under the stars," as the army would say. A stable where one could bunk down next to the animals was an unexpected but welcome blessing.

I'll never forget lying down next to a stall with a lively horse, my suitcase serving as a pillow. A little straw under my neck and shoulder should have made it less painful. I might have slept a little if my neighborly horse had stopped stamping his feet in discontent or if the rats had left us alone. As it was, I spent the whole night hitting the stall with a stick to chase the rats away. I was far too scared to sleep!

After a painful night, we got back on the road.

Engraved in my memory is the beautiful road ahead that reminded me of the Alps, with its long hill of unspoiled scenery. Pine trees lined both sides of the road and reached for miles up to the skies. A heaven of black forest.

There were no troops on that road. All we could see was a mass of evacuees, the pines, and the sun trying to peer through the trees. But sounds of war permeated the air. We had dismounted our bikes because the hill was too steep and everyone was struggling to reach the top, when suddenly the familiar sound of the diving German stukas came roaring from the distance. We instantly dropped our bikes, jumped over the huge ravine and dove into a crater made by a previous bomb.

Tuck, tuck, tuck, tuck, tuck...went the low-flying aircrafts, strafing the refugees. The planes would regain altitude, then return for the next attack. When it was over, we crawled out of our hole to attend to the wounded and dying who had not escaped the carnage.

After one of these attacks, I found a little redheaded girl, about thirteen, lying on the side of the road in the fetal position. She looked exactly like my younger sister. Screaming, I ran over to find that it was not Cécile. I touched her face and hands to make her respond. Her body was still warm, but she was dead. Struck with horror, I screamed obscenities at our enemy. Agony and anger were creating rage in my heart. *How could God let this happen to a beautiful young girl and all these innocent people?*

By the time we reached Beauvais, the front line of battle was closing in on us. We were being bombed and machine-gunned nonstop. I can't remember how long it took for the Germans to catch up with us. It seemed at least four days and nights. The enemy was now at our heels. It was time to take cover and stop this useless race.

Civilian exodus. Belgians fleeing to France.

akg-images London

05 **German Overtake**

South of Beauvais, France, and apparently a short distance from Paris, Mademoiselle and I stopped at a farm to seek lodging and drink. It was a good-sized farm, built in the eighteenth century, with a center courtyard surrounded by the farmer's dwelling, stables and barns—all in the form of a square. What we found was a conglomeration of humanity— evacuees of all ages and backgrounds and a massive number of the French army in retreat. The farmer, overwhelmed and annoyed with the demands of refugees from the north, told us that we could stay long enough to help distribute fresh milk to the French soldiers.

Entrance to a Belgian farm similar to that in Beauvais.

Our host farmer took pity on them. He had milked his cows and placed the huge cans, destined for the creamery, at the edge of the street instead. We were to fill the cup of every soldier passing by.

These troops were only too happy to take the aluminum cups off their belts and reach for a drink. A great number of them were Algerians who were tired, hungry and ready to give up. I'll never forget the contrast between these poorly-equipped defenders who were ready to capitulate, and the highly disciplined, well-supplied German aggressors that we later encountered. The sight of the French Army gave us no hope for halting the enemy invasion or winning the war. We knew that by now, it was over for us. The German frontline was at our doorstep.

The farm in Beauvais (likeness)—the homestead wing.

French officers placed a cannon in the courtyard of the farm. German troops did the same within a short distance, and the battle was on. Artillery fire was raging, shells were flying over the rooftops, airborne debris and orders screamed from every direction. On the outer side of the farm compound, the farmer had dug a hole in the ground, deep enough for his family to stand in. It had a few dirt steps to go down and a piece of corrugated aluminum on top, which served as the roof; dirt and stones were piled on top as camouflage.

As the first cannon shell exploded nearby, we stormed the makeshift shelter, our only refuge, and the battle raged on. Huddled in our hole—father, mother, grandmother, two children, Mademoiselle and I—we silently listened to the chaos above, with indescribable fear. We could hear and see parts of the roof and bricks falling down the steps into the shelter. To escape injury, Mademoiselle and I moved closer to the family.

Calls for help and screams were heard, but no one could venture out. Bullets were flying, bombs were falling, and cannons were furiously shooting, as debris fell out of the sky. It was an hour out of hell! Once in a

Exit from the courtyard to the bunker (likeness).

while I could hear one of the children crying; the cries were quickly muffled by the little girl's mother. I started to pray in a whisper. The farmer joined in my prayers, and so did Grandma. After what I thought was an hour or so, the battle ceased. There was a short moment of total silence. An eerie silence, a deadly silence! One had visions of dead bodies all over the fields. Where could all those soldiers have gone? We were paralyzed with fear. Then, a strange, powerful noise was heard. It sounded almost like a cavalry unit. I still have not been able to figure it out. My hearing told me that there were horses galloping on the side road. But never did I see one. Suddenly all shooting had stopped. We heard people talking and tanks and heavy equipment rolling by on the highway. I found out later that the Germans were through Beauvais and on their way to Paris.

With my heart in my throat, I whispered, "The Germans are here!" The farmer looked at me in despair and said, "You are the only one of us who speaks German! Please tell them that we have no weapons and that there are children and family here." The poor man was so scared that his voice and whole body trembled. From Mademoiselle there was no sound. She looked frozen! The rest of the family was crying, ever so fearful that the Germans would simply shoot everyone down in the dark hole.

I gingerly walked up the dirt steps. By now, they were full of debris from the top of the damaged farm house. As I reached the top of the stairs, I was heard by a German soldier who, in a flash, had his gun pointed at my chest and screamed, "Halt!"

In the best German I could muster, hands above my head as a sign of abdication, I yelled, "I am German. I came to visit my family who is hiding in this bunker. There are no weapons down there. I give you my word!"

Everyone was ordered out of the shelter. I whispered in French to our hosts about the lie that I had told. A soldier was ordered to search the bunker. The family was ordered back into the house to stay. We were stunned by the absence of French troops. The tableau of the corpse-strewn battlefield that I had imagined was not there. *Where had they all gone?*

I was immediately accosted by a German officer who wanted me to translate his inquiry of an Algerian prisoner of war. I cautiously asked the officer a simple question in French to make sure that my German aggressor did not speak French, then deliberately twisted the information given to me by the prisoner. The officer then informed me of my "duty as a German citizen." He declared, "You are needed in the war effort and will be the interpreter for the Commandant at his headquarters in Beauvais."

I negotiated with him over some badly needed sleep. We had not slept the last three nights, so he accepted my plea for one night of rest at the farm. The officer called a Gestapo (member of the German State Police, organized in 1933 by the Nazis), who arrived on a huge motorcycle with a sidecar and told him to pick me up at 9 a.m. the next morning. He was ordered to take me to the German military headquarters that they had set up in Beauvais, located only a few kilometers from where we were.

I had to tell Mademoiselle my bad news.

* * * * *

06 **Deadly Pastures**

In the heat of the battle, my entire exchange with the officer had taken place with such rapidity that Madeleine looked totally flabbergasted. The thought of losing her young companion to the Gestapo at nine the next morning was frightening. She did not speak German and had not understood much of my conversation nor the trickery that I had engaged in to buy time.

At that point I decided that we should at least pretend to settle down in one of the stables for the night, knowing that we would stay only as long as these German officers remained in the area. We would need to escape by detouring Beauvais before morning. My heart was beating with fear as my brain planned our escape. I thought of how my father would always encourage me to be strong and courageous. I looked at my lovely blue hat and knew that it would have to be left behind. It was far too noticeable, even in the dark of night, to wear on our clandestine escape. I thought of Maman, and I hated to leave her gift there. I hid it in a corner of the stable, under the hay, hoping that the farmer's daughter would find it and love it as much as I did.

Night was falling rapidly, and neither sleep nor work for the enemy was on our agenda. Finding a way to get out of there without being detected was our only concern. By now Mademoiselle knew what was at stake, but she had no plan; she just followed me. I was sorry for her and felt responsible for her safety.

It must have been sometime after midnight when we decided that it was time to make our move. German troops were still marching rapidly on the road leading to Paris. The officer who had given me the command to report to the headquarters in Beauvais was long gone with his troops, and the Gestapo that he had summoned to fetch me the next morning remained at headquarters where he was to take me.

Our main objective was to avoid German confrontation at all costs. I had lied about my nationality and could not risk meeting the German patrol, or the Gestapo, again. If arrested, I was sure that I could be shot as a spy.

Most roads were loaded with German troops and could not be used. We waited for a break in the military convoy, quickly crossed the road, climbed up a short bank, and carried our bikes into the field. Trees helped camouflage us from the bright moonlight as we silently crept along the hedges and further up through the field.

After what seemed an eternity of hard work, we were out of sight of what we thought would be enemy-occupied highways. The troops could still be heard advancing, and fear of being detected and shot in the back motivated us to carry out the horrendous task of fleeing deep into the farmland.

The field was lush with green grass, but very uneven. We had to carry our bikes by the central bar to keep our balance. At times, we would take a brief stop to reposition a hand and improve circulation. A few cows were grazing, and many were lying upside down in the field, their stiff legs pointed to the sky. There was a stench of death from all directions. Horses and cows had not avoided the bullets.

We were laboring our way through this former battlefield when, suddenly, there was a ray of hope in the distance.

"Bless us," I said to Mademoiselle. "The moon is showing a farm on the horizon. Do you see it? There is a little gate at the end of this field and probably a country road for us to ride on."

In a discouraged tone of voice came the reply, "I can see none of it! I am simply too exhausted to see anything."

We finally reached the end of the pasture and, by the light of the moon, saw a little gate with what looked like a huge sign hanging on the outside. I presumed that there was writing on the other side, so that people coming from the farm, or traveling the dirt road, would see it. Suddenly, my heart was in my throat! I felt in imminent danger. Not wanting to panic my friend with my thoughts, I asked her to tread very slowly and carefully the last few steps. Cautiously putting one foot in front of the other, I lifted our bikes over the fence and told her to climb over without taking any unnecessary steps. Poor Madeleine, while obediently and silently doing what I asked, wanted to know what had gotten into me. *She has never displayed much strength,* I thought. She was willing to follow directions like a child, to follow any orders. I felt forced to take charge of the situation.

The sign was clearly written in German, and said: *NICHT EINTRATEN, MINED* [DO NOT ENTER! MINED]!

We fell to our knees, embraced, and thanked God and our guardian angels for having saved us from suffering the same fate as all the animals in that field. We felt as though we had conquered the world. We were alive and ready to run from the barking watchdog in the farmhouse.

Newly invigorated by the miracle that God had just bestowed on us, we ventured down a small dirt road to the next village. By the time the sun rose, we were far enough from Beauvais, and joined with thousands of refugees going back to Belgium, leaving the Germans behind to fight and continue their carnage of Europe. It took three more days of hard riding, sleeping under the stars, and depending on the good will and hospitality of strangers, to get us back to Andenne.

* * * * *

Finally, our last day of travel arrived! We would reach Andenne by nightfall. Full of joy and anticipation, but also fear of what we might find, our tired bodies forged ahead with a new surge of adrenaline. Disregarding hunger and exhaustion, we pedaled faster than usual. We looked as though we were in a race, dashing for the finish line.

"Oh, yes!" Madeleine cried out, "The villa is standing. They did not hit it!" We approached and saw that the structure did seem undamaged; its windows and rooftops looked intact. That relief lasted only a moment. Madeleine entered the house from the side porch where she had been awaiting my arrival.

She opened the broken-down door without a key, stepped inside and let out a scream of despair. Before I knew why, she had burst into tears, and ran to her private study in back of the formal living room.

The villa was totally ransacked; not one thing remained untouched. I stood there in shock. The beautiful sculptured marble fireplace was un-recognizable.

Angry and indignant, I screamed insults and climbed over the broken Limoges china and the Belgian Val Saint-Lambert crystal, in pieces all over the floor. Oriental rugs did not escape the cruel destruction; they were cut and burnt irreparably.

Neighbors rushed over to greet us and welcome us back. They told the story of how the Germans had gone into any homes where the people had fled, and punished them by vandalizing their empty houses. They told of German army vehicles that pulled up in front of our villa to empty the wine cellar. "They were all drunk," said François, our elderly neighbor who had been too old to evacuate. They stole everything they wanted, and what they could not take, they destroyed by using the butt of their guns. The drawers and doors of the magnificent Louis XV furniture were reduced to firewood.

Mademoiselle Madeleine was in her study, sobbing uncontrollably. I wanted to share her pain with her. I slowly pushed the door ajar and saw my devastated lady reclined on what had been her elegant chaise lounge. The upholstery, soft pink and green Belgian tapestry, had been slashed from top to bottom and partially torn off the chair. I was instantly reminded of a painting of a nude sleeping beauty in distress. I cannot remember the artist, nor where I saw this work of art that had so impressed me, but I recalled it instantly when faced with this live horrible scene.

I wanted to rush over and take her in my arms, but I discretely backed out, to respect her moment of private mourning. She should not be disturbed. I stood out of her view, in silence and in tears, and waited. The picture of her desecrated house reminded me that the war was far from over. *Oh Lord!* I thought. *What of my parents and my family? Would I witness this same ordeal at home?* I suddenly felt that if they were just alive, I would be thankful to God. "Just alive, Lord," I prayed. "Let me just find them alive." For a moment all the destruction around me became unimportant.

Madeleine struggled to regain her composure. I quietly ventured into the room, put my arms around her, and whispered, "Mademoiselle Madeleine, we are alive! We are alive!" She stared blankly at me. She was crushed. I thought of Monsieur Jean and wished that he were here to help.

"We must rise," I said to her. "We must make this home livable for Monsieur Jean when he returns." Nothing more was spoken. No words could describe our emotions. We tried to find solace in the gift of life that God had so graciously given us.

* * * * *

Arriving in Andenne was only the first step toward my goal of getting home. I was scared and restless and wanted to run to Montzen, where I hoped to find my people alive. Not knowing what had happened to them was unbearable.

I started working furiously to restore the house to a livable condition where Madeleine could sleep in a clean bed, eat from her dishes, or just sit and look out the window at her beautiful garden, rather than being faced by her ravished house. We cleaned the kitchen, her bedroom, and the study—her favorite hideaway overlooking a flower bed.

On the second day of our return, I decided to visit her best friend, Mademoiselle Courti, to ask for her help. She and her brother had a big farm and offered immediate assistance. They loaded my bike with enough food to last Madeleine for a month. They insisted that I take one of their watchdogs along for Madeleine's protection while I was gone home to Montzen. Her friend assured me that Madeleine would be well looked after. The Courti family, brother and sister, would visit her the day after my departure and take charge.

I soon was able to bid my lady *au revoir.* I promised to be back as soon as my family no longer needed my help. I set out on foot, knowing the difficulties ahead. Phones were out of order. Transportation was scarce. Trains and buses were seriously hampered by bombings and the devastation of war; few were running toward my hometown.

No one knew what the situation was at the German border since the invasion, and no one could give me accurate information.

I walked to the railroad station in Andenne. It was closed! With my backpack loaded with sandwiches, a bottle of water, and some makeshift rainwear, I was prepared for the time that it would take to travel approximately 60 kilometers (37.5 miles) on foot to find my parents. I kept my eyes open for any gentle soul who might give me a ride even a short distance at a time. Safety didn't enter my mind. The Germans were going south, fighting their way into France. I was going north. The cities and highways were overrun by enemy military, so I traveled through the countryside as much as possible.

Once, I accepted a ride, sitting precariously on the end of a hay wagon and dangling my feet over the end. I enjoyed these respites, for they gave my poor feet a rest. At the end of the ride, the compassionate farmer waved me on, saying, "I think the buses are running up ahead." This ended up being wishful thinking!

I often found myself standing on the side of a road, not knowing in which direction to go, and called on my guardian angel to come to my aid. I would remember Maman's words when we left for school: *"Be good, and go with your guardian angel."*

Not that I was always such an obedient child! Sometimes I must have made my guardian angel frown. Once, on our way back from school, I knocked down a few nice-looking apples from one of the farmer's trees and shared them with my buddies until we saw the angry farmer running after us, swinging what looked like a shotgun in his hand. He followed us all the way home and talked to my father! I will not tell what my punishment was, only that I have never forgotten the incident!

In obedience to Maman I prayed, and here and there I would see a bus and take a short but heavenly ride that brought me closer to home.

Within a few kilometers of Montzen, I was stopped by a German soldier of the Wehrmacht and told to show my passport to enter into Germany. I informed him that I had no desire to go to Germany but was heading to Montzen, in Belgium.

"So, you speak German," he said. "Then you will be much at home in Montzen, which has now become a part of Germany. The border, Fraulein, has been moved into Belgium, and you are now a German citizen." (See the map on page xvii.) My ID showed that I was from Montzen, and my interrogator was only too happy to let me return to my hometown. I stood there in shock, utterly confused. I did not know that they had moved the border and annexed our hometown. I turned away from him and burst into tears.

The invasion had been so sudden that my family had had no time to run. While they were rapidly packing clothes to escape from the invaders, each child making a bundle out of a pillowcase to carry his or her possessions, the German Infantry and Panzer Division were crawling all over the land.

Soldiers had stormed into our little store, telling my parents to stop preparing to evacuate. "Too late," they said to Maman: "Calm down and stay home and take care of your children. You will not be harmed." What a different tone from World War I, when men in our village were shot in retaliation for a fallen German officer.

I arrived home and found my family in good health. We were stunned and elated to find each other, all of us alive! We hugged, and tears of joy were shed. To find my family alive gave a whole new dimension to my existence. Home at last, I had a clean bed to lay my head on, and food from the farms around us. Papa's garden was well-stocked with plenty of vegetables to eat. I recognized these simple pleasures as true gifts from heaven.

I was home alright, but I could feel that nothing was the same! Major changes had taken place. The lady who used to come on Mondays to help with our huge laundry and on Tuesdays to do the ironing, was no longer able to come. On Thursday afternoons, the seamstress, Madame Jadot, who used to come to make our clothes, teach the girls to mend socks, and repair garments, was ill and made no promises for the future. As a teenager, I had always liked that day, and loved the lessons Madame Jadot gave us. There was no school on Thursday afternoon. We went to school Saturday morning instead.

In one room on the third floor, Papa had installed a long table with a sewing machine at the end. The seamstress would place a small pile of socks that needed mending, a wooden egg, needles with special mercerized thread, and small scissors on the table in front of each one of us. We girls were taught to mend socks without leaving tight lumps that would hurt the feet. The rule was that when we came back from school on Thursdays, we'd eat our lunch and go upstairs for the sewing lesson. All items had to be repaired before we were free to go to the garden to play.

I was tempted more than once to pull the hole of the socks a little tighter, making the hole smaller so it would take less time to mend. But there was Maman, who always took the time to check our work. She'd examine my brother's mended wool sock and point out the lump I had fashioned under the foot to close the hole, grab a pair of scissors, and cut out my bad job, which made the hole bigger than before. Then I would have to re-do it correctly. Crying did not help! Maman would ask one question: "Can you be proud of this?" She instilled pride in her children by demanding that jobs be well done. Honesty in our work and pride in our best efforts were always emphasized.

After my evacuation experiences, life looked sweet in the heart of the family. There were many more chores to be done, but we were happy to be together again, sharing the newly imposed struggle of our lives.

Little did I know that my stay in this warm, secure environment would be of short duration.

* * * * *

09 **Church Bells to Bullets**
Occupation and Life under German Rule—Montzen1940

As I savored the love found with my family, I discovered what really had been lost and how my parents' lives had changed. Freedom seemed to be a thing of the past. All decisions were now made by the new "regime."

Our little store had been put under German control. We were allowed to buy and sell according to regulations imposed by the occupying forces. Food stamps were strictly enforced.

German citizenship and military service were forced on people from Eupen, Malmedy, and Saint Vith, all within the region that had been German before World War I. In addition, any male inhabitant living in the other ten "newly-annexed" boroughs, or who had even a remote relative of German descent, was drafted into the Wehrmacht and sent to the front, fighting against his own people and those he grew up with. Rules and laws had changed. This part of Belgium was not just occupied by Germany, but was annexed by—made part of—Germany! All Belgian school teachers were fired. German teachers were brought in to replace them, and began to teach all classes in German. Before the war we had learned German as a second language, starting in third grade. Now, it became the primary language!

My younger brothers and sisters went back to school and were forced under penalty to greet the teachers with a raised arm and a loud "Heil Hitler." My brothers Hubert and Theo tell stories about the different punishments they endured when they banded together in disobedience and refused to utter this greeting. One cold winter day, which they never forgot, a group of them were made to stand outside without winter coats, in raised-arm salute. They shivered and rattled their teeth before the teacher brought them back inside. They were not discouraged, however, and started another protest within the next couple of days.

Young people of fourteen and older in our annexed region were forced to leave school and go to work for the war effort. It was obligatory to carry our work-cards at all times. Now people were told to gather all metals, pots and pans, gold and silver, aluminum and steel, and deliver them to our little station to be loaded on trains and shipped to Germany to make am-munition. Even our church bells were taken out of the steeple. Only one bell was left to announce religious services. The rest were sent to Antwerp and loaded on ships to be transported to Germany. They would be melted down for bullets! The Belgian authorities were happy to find them still sitting in the port of Antwerp when the war was over, and returned them to the steeple in the church of Montzen, a small but significant act of defiance.

I was home alright, but nothing was the same!

My father's fear that I would be picked up by the German authorities still seemed very justified. I was told to return to Andenne and to Mademoiselle, and to stay there until further notice. Papa felt that since that part of Belgium was occupied, but not annexed like Montzen, my chances of escaping the enemy draft would be better.

* * * * *

10 **Uncle Alphonse**

Complying with my father's wish for my return to Andenne was no small feat. Under the new regime, I would need a passport to get out of "annexed Germany." Asking for permission would automatically make me a target. Patriotic young "Germans" did not leave the country; they all worked for the war effort! I would be considered a traitor to the Fatherland, a runaway to be punished with hard labor. Another avenue had to be considered.

Maman's sister, Tante Martine, and her husband, Uncle Alphonse, lived on a dirt road in the middle of farmland, about an hour's walk from our home. The train from Montzen to Hombourg, where they lived, passed directly by their house. Every time a train was due, bells would ring loudly. Uncle Alphonse, who was the gatekeeper, would fly out of the house to close the gates where the trains crossed over the dirt road. He was a short and funny little man, exuberant and cheerful as he whistled his way to and from the gates.

As a family, we used to love to visit them on our Sunday afternoon outings. He and Tante [Aunt] Martine and their children would welcome us with open arms. Uncle would play his flute, tell jokes, and sing folk songs. We would play games while waiting expectantly for a train to come by. When a clamor of ringing bells would commence, Uncle Alphonse would jump up like a *Hampelmann* [German: leprechaun]. He always reminded me of a leprechaun flying out the door to put down those gates.

We children would rush out into the fenced garden about sixty feet from the rails and watch him go into action. We would wave at the people sitting at the windows of the train and wait for passengers to wave back.

Later, during the war, Uncle Alphonse and Tante Martine played a major role in the work of the Resistance. They learned the names and whereabouts

The cement foundation, all that remains of Uncle Alphonse and Tante Martine's house. On the right, the old railroad crossing.

of all the German guards patrolling the newly-imposed German border. If a patriot wanted to get out of Germany to flee the area, Uncle could tell him the approximate time of the changing of the guards. He knew "when" they passed by on patrol, rifles over their shoulders and ferocious-looking German shepherds in tow. At the same time, fearless Tante Martine would serve the guards coffee and cookies to distract them. She would seat them away from the kitchen window, and even daringly dash out the door to wave a patriot over the border while Uncle Alphonse kept them entertained. Today, their son, Fernand, still marvels at his courageous parents. He chuckles when he tells of his mother's bold exploits. Uncle Alphonse, on the other hand, might have been more scared than his wife, but seemed to know every one of the guards and their dogs by name. I felt that he would be my safest ticket out of Montzen. When I showed up and asked him for help to pass over the border into Belgium without this newly required passport, he knew exactly how to proceed and be safe.

When the time came for me to leave, Uncle went out to the garden and, as usual, whistled a happy tune that would make the German guard dogs bark. This little trick would identify their location, and tell Uncle if it was safe to go. That was how I got over the forbidden border and to Andenne without being arrested. From that time on, visits with my parents under such circumstances were impossible. They would be too dangerous as long as the enemy occupied our country. Mademoiselle and her brother, Monsieur Jean, who had returned from the Belgian front unharmed, were very happy to see me back. I stayed at the villa until 1942 when I received word from Papa that I was drafted and had to report back to Montzen. I never understood why it took the Germans so long to catch up with me. They obviously never found out that I had left Montzen again.

Life in Andenne with Mademoiselle was tolerable as long as the German troops from the nearby military barracks left us alone. They would march up and down our road in perfect formation, singing German songs at the top of their voices. Their performances were designed to encourage their own troops and to promote happiness and optimism in the Belgian people, but we would close the windows and doors to show disdain. Their collective voices were so strong, however, that we could hear them anyway. I think those of us who knew some German learned all the songs, whether we liked them or not.

At this time food was strictly rationed. The bread we could buy was usually some dark mass that would stick to the knife when we tried to cut it.

After the war, my oldest sister, Bertha, told the story of the day my brother Joseph, then twenty-two, claimed that they were being made to eat glue. She said that he got so angry that, to prove his point, he threw a piece of bread to the ceiling. To everyone's shock, the bread stuck up there just as Joseph had predicted it would.

Mademoiselle's dear friend let us get butter and homemade bread from her farm. The catch was that the farmer always needed help and wanted to be repaid generously.

We were taught by my parents that we should not refuse help when it was needed, so I volunteered to churn the butter in a dark cellar at two o'clock in the morning, when it was safe to take the risk.

We waited long into the night to make sure that all German patrols had passed by and that no strange dogs were snooping around the farm. Down in the dark room that felt like a dungeon, I would grab the big handle of the barrel full of cream, and turn, turn, turn, always keeping an ear cocked for the slightest noise or sound of steps from the outside. During this chore, someone was assigned a nightly vigil in the kitchen. The fear that the patrols might return was always present. I could no longer hear well while doing the work, and I felt that an hour or more of churning this heavy barrel was punishment enough for my body. I had to trust the person upstairs to keep watch.

Suddenly, a sigh of relief! The liquid would start lumping together as the butter was forming. The barrel would became heavy and difficult to turn. It made sounds like thunder! Soon it would be over. By now, I'd have run out of prayers, and my Hail Mary's had become meaningless words.

We spent the rest of the night at the farm but, early in the morning, Madeleine and I would return to our villa with a kilo of fresh butter, two loaves of fresh bread, and some fresh eggs. This was our well-earned reward. Our only hope was not to be stopped by a guard on the way home and lose our precious staples.

During the spring, in an effort to survive with home-grown food, Mademoiselle and I had painstakingly planted a vegetable garden. We planned on preserving the harvest for the next winter. Food was scarce and everyone was trying to avoid starvation by canning what they could grow. German patrols controlled all farm production and tried to stop farmers from cheating on the portion allowed for their own consumption. Failing to declare any amount of food or butter, as dictated by the authorities, meant severe punishment. All goods harvested above the allowed portion were to be handed over to the authorities.

One morning, while I was cleaning the bedroom, I saw two German soldiers picking vegetables from our garden. They must have seen me through the trees because they grabbed their huge basket, jumped down the embankment and went out into the street. Soon I heard a truck leaving the side of our property.

Mademoiselle ran to the garden and saw that they had taken a huge harvest of leeks, almost all of our big heads of lettuce, and the entire harvest of pole beans that were just ready to be preserved. My poor friend just stood there crying, "They have stolen it all!"

Not I! Indignation and anger at their arrogance and thievery took hold of me! I ran down to the yard, ripped off my apron, jumped on my bike, and pedaled as fast as I could to the military barracks, about one kilometer down the road. I threw my bike against the first building that looked like an office, stomped into a hallway, and passed a guard who yelled *Halt* at the top of his voice.

I stopped instantly for fear he might shoot me if I did not. I turned abruptly toward him and screamed in perfect German, "I must see your Commandant. Now!"

The man was stunned. He let out a nervous laugh and explained, "No civilian can see the Commandant, Fraulein."

I countered loudly but politely, "Yes, I can. It is urgent. I will see him, now."

The bewildered young guard knocked at a heavy door, opened it, and stood back, motioning me in.

There I was, facing a tall, handsome German officer who grabbed his *kepi* [officer's hat], put it on his head as though he wanted to be in full uniform before engaging in conversation, and offered, "Now Fraulein, what can I do for you?"

I noticed that I did not get a reprimand for not greeting him with "Heil Hitler," and answered with a "Good day" greeting, "*Guten Tag, Herr Commandant,*" even though I had no idea if he really was the Commander!

"Your soldiers," I said, "have just stolen all the vegetables from our garden!"

At my pronouncement of "stealing," his whole demeanor changed. He jumped up from his big chair and declared in a very loud voice that "Germans do not steal!"

"They confiscated our food for an entire winter without giving us a requisition," I maintained just as loudly. "What should we call this?" I was careful not to repeat the dreaded word "stealing," and just waited.

He calmly sat down and wrote out a requisition to be cashed at their office, for far more money than we were owed. He handed it to me and said, "We call that WAR, Fraulein!" He raised his arm and saluted me with "Heil Hitler," which I did not return.

I left his presence with a *Danke* and a feeling that I had just met an honest German.

* * * * *

11 **Jump, Drop, and Roll**
The First Leap of Faith—1942

By 1942 my father had sent this message: "Return to Montzen to acknowledge your draft papers." I was being deported to Danzig, Germany, to work in an ammunition factory. The document specified that failure to report at the train station meant imprisonment for fathers or for the main breadwinners.

At that time Hitler ordered a massive deportation of all available young people from occupied countries. Young German men were needed in the military and would be replaced in their factory jobs by deportees from Belgium, France and perhaps other occupied countries. My oldest brother Joseph was hiding in the cellar of our house. Bertha, my oldest sister, was working as a seamstress for the Germans. She was afraid of being drafted and deported, so she volunteered to work for them. There was no question in my mind about what I was going to do. The idea of ending up in a deportation camp, working for Hitler's war against my own people, turned my stomach. The anger I felt at Hitler's arrogance was all-consuming, and helped me engage in whatever dangerous venture it took to bring about his defeat.

After my tearful goodbyes with the rest of the family, Papa walked me halfway to the station. He gave me advice about how to respond when confronted by German guards: "Do not ever show fear to an enemy who confronts you. Faced with this situation, use your best German intelligently. A few words spoken loudly will have more effect and better results." I told Papa that I would always remember his words of wisdom.

Before both of us became too emotional, I revealed, "Papa, my secret to you alone is that I will report at the station, but will not stay on the train to Germany.

I've heard people talking about a certain spot where one can jump off and escape deportation, and I am determined to do just that." I told him with confidence that I intended to get off the train about a mile down the tracks, go to my uncle, a priest in Liège, and join the underground. To my surprise, he did not seem upset, and did not try to discourage me. He acted as though he already knew! He simply advised, "Be careful," and *"Bon courage."* Papa never said, "I love you," but his strong hug told me so. It was time to go!

The viaduct connecting Belgium to Aachen, Germany.
Above, far left: the spot where I jumped off the train.
Bottom: the viaduct after the war, blown up by the Germans.

I reported to a mean-looking guard at the door of our little station's waiting room. My name was checked off the list, and I was told to proceed through the station to board the train.

I chose a car in the center of the train and claimed a seat near the door.

I overheard some passengers say that a few people had previously jumped off the train where it made a slight bend before getting onto the viaduct leading to Aachen, Germany. Though armed German guards watched from the first and last cars, I heard two young men whispering about the place where the train would have to slow down considerably.

"We jump, drop and roll down into a ball before the first farm," I heard one say.

This patriot, whom I had never seen before, looked unafraid and determined. He inspired me to be the same. As soon as I could get his attention, without uttering one word, I motioned to him that I was coming too. He understood instantly.

Within minutes, the train came to what I thought was a slight bend on the rail bed. It slowed almost to a stop. The young man whom I had heard, and now understood was the leader, slipped out of his seat and headed for the door of the train. A discreet sign of his hand and three more of us followed. Within a split second we were rolling, one after the other, tightly wrapped in our winter coats, with our arms tucked around our bodies, holding our sacks of meager belongings. Down the embankment, through tall, green grass we went. The German guards on the back of the train never saw us; no shots were fired. We lay there motionless at the bottom of the hill until the last train had cleared the area. Our brave leader tried to rise but had injured his leg; he thought it was broken. We carried him to a nearby farmhouse. They would care for him there while we fled our separate ways toward the new border of Belgium.

Within minutes we set out on foot in whatever direction each had in mind. We did not know or trust each other. The object was to get to the other side of the newly imposed border of Belgium without getting stopped by the German border guards. It seemed that the draft had not yet been as severely implemented in the occupied area as it was in the annexed part of the country.

I soon found myself alone and headed toward the only farmland that I knew, Uncle Alfonse's. Dear Uncle Alphonse! He and his wife, Tante Martine, would know how to get me back over the border and on my way to hiding. They risked their lives so many times to help escapees get out of harm's way. They saw this as a duty to their countrymen. Their home was a village away, and I was ready to walk the kilometers it took to reach it and hopefully get to Liège and Uncle Hubert's Rectory. Uncle Hubert was Papa's brother and was pastor of Saint Bartholomew's parish. He was a good and devout priest, and I would be safe with him! That was my hope.

* * * * *

12 **The Long Road to Hiding**

I walked through the fields from one farm to the next, taking only small dirt roads, watching for the border guards, listening for a warning from barking dogs. I don't know how, but by the grace of God or my guardian angel, I found myself on a blacktop road, far from my hometown. Here and there a bus would pass, going in the direction of Liège. I was tempted to hop on, but needed to walk much further before having the courage to do so. I had to think twice about such a dangerous move. Most Belgian people talk to each other on the bus; for them it's a social hour. If I were silent, I would certainly arouse suspicion. If I spoke, I would want to say very little, and then would have to lie about my whereabouts. So I walked on and found a lovely secluded place to spent a short night under the stars.

The next day, I spotted a bus stop. It was well marked—Herstal, Liège. With my heart beating faster in my chest, I waited my turn and stepped up to the front door. In Belgium, passengers board by the front door of the bus and exit by the middle door or toward the back. The first thing to do was to make sure there were no German military on the bus. I swiftly glanced at an empty seat near the back door. If anyone dressed in a gray-blue Wehrmacht uniform were to enter at the front, I'd be able to escape through the back. I was scared out of my wits that I'd be picked up, but determined to adopt a low profile and go on.

The bus driver, a patriot no doubt, was a kind but aggressive middle-aged man who observed everyone coming onboard. I don't know how, but he seemed to know that I was a runaway from the German border, the area of Belgium annexed to Germany. Somehow, he figured out that I was in danger. I was head down, getting my change to pay him, when he asked for my destination. He must have seen that I was hesitant to tell him. Not waiting for my change, he put his hand over mine, making it look as though he was taking my money. He slipped the coins back into my hand, whispering authoritatively, "*Descendez au troisième arrêt* [Get off at the third stop]."

When the bus arrived at the third stop, he quietly announced in his deep voice, "*Troisième arrêt.*" I got off the bus, took a side street and disappeared. While deciding which way to go, I realized that I was heading toward some kind of barracks. German trucks and military personnel were all over the place. IDs were being checked on street corners. I needed time to think.

I slipped into a *traiteur* (a market for readymade food) where I was the only customer, and bought a nice fresh *pistolet*, a delicious Belgian hard-crusted roll, with a slice of cheese and a piece of the elite *jambon d'Ardennes* (smoked ham of the Ardennes). I headed back out to the street, but this time in the opposite direction. I munched heartily on what was my first bite of the day and reached my destination without having to show my ID once. Thanks to my patriotic bus driver, who knew the whereabouts of the German encampment, I made my escape with a few rewards: a full stomach, the satisfaction of being free to fight for my homeland, and the pride of succeeding in this unforgettable journey by myself.

Papa would be shocked to know how his daughter found refuge that night. I traveled across fields and slept a few hours in an open hangar, surrounded by bales of hay piled high on either side, making a secure hideaway for this scared and lonely traveler. A blue translucent corrugated roof gave the only available light, and kept the hay dry in the event of rain. I woke up with the sun rising in the distance, birds flying in and out nonstop, and a few curious cows checking me out. I started talking to them as I usually do when I am around animals. They just stared at me and stupidly mooed away.

Papa couldn't know what a rich experience it turned out to be, what a heavenly peaceful place it was. For a brief moment I forgot my fear and wished I could stay there for a while. Today, I still think of it affectionately.

Lush Belgian farmland.

.

13 **Liège at Last**

I arrived at Uncle Hubert's doorstep at the rectory of Saint Bartholomew in Liège by nightfall. The light was on in his study, and I knew that he was deep in prayer. He used to call me his favorite niece and was probably asking the Lord to protect me during my forty-seven kilometer journey. Uncle knew that I was en route, but had no idea when I would arrive.

I could not have landed in a more heartwarming place. My father's older brother was a kind, generous man. He loved his parish and cared very much for his people, especially those families who were less fortunate and needed help. A learned man, with a broad interest in music, literature and the arts, he had the respect and admiration of all.

After a hearty welcome, he handed me over to Marguerite, a sweet Jewish lady whose husband had fallen into the hands of the Germans and ended up in Dachau, one of the concentration camps where Jews were interned or put to death. Uncle had taken her in with her twelve-year-old daughter, to save them from the Nazis. Marguerite was acting as the housekeeper's helper, and had prepared a warm meal for me that I devoured with gusto. I was then ushered to the bathroom where she gave me a healing foot massage, and then helped me into a nice, warm bath. Such luxurious care I had never experienced before. A few words of instruction given by Uncle Hubert about what to do if the German patrols should ring the doorbell at night, and I sank into a delicious sleep on the third floor of the house.

The next day I found out what a hectic and dangerous place this could be. There was no peace! Phone calls from parishioners in need of help were constant. Every accident, illness or death seemed to end up on the steps of the rectory. Many times the phone and the doorbell rang at the same time with the same sense of urgency. Every conversation and peaceful moment was interrupted.

I can still see my uncle going to his small garden, enclosed by the walls of the massive medieval church. Every day at noon, he would steal that time when the church bells were sounding the *Angelus*. Standing still or walking slowly, he'd open his breviary, read the scripture, and say the prayers of the hours. From what I saw, aside from church services, this was his only restful moment of the day.

He always ate his dinner immediately after prayers, and alone. He needed that time to concentrate on solving the problems so pervasive in his parish.

At that time, Uncle Hubert was *le doyen* [the Dean], who oversaw a cluster of churches. He should have had a vicar to assist him, but Uncle was alone most of the time. There were no days off, let alone vacations. It was war!

We may have been in French-speaking Belgium, but it was occupied by the enemy, and it could be more dangerous there than it was at home with my parents. Here, every sound of the doorbell made us jump with fear. There was a hush surrounding us like a dark cloud over the house.

Uncle Hubert was involved with hiding Jewish people, so when the doorbell rang, we never knew what we would face. It could be a parishioner needing assistance, a new escapee, or the dreaded Gestapo. Oh yes, the Gestapo! They were everywhere; if not physically on our heels, then mentally on our minds. We were very aware that by this time—1942—the enemy, especially the Gestapo, had dropped all pretense of being civil and were shooting people on the spot, for wrong answers or trivial offenses against their regime.

At night, we slept partially dressed to make a quick escape through the dormer window, if necessary. The German soldiers were patrolling the streets. They walked slowly, rifles over their shoulders, clicking their heels on the cobblestones. Their boots were heeled with a half-moon piece of iron that rang out like a deadly alarm on the pavements. From far away we could hear them coming. We would jump out of bed, throw on the rest of our clothes, and silently wait for a stop in their steps.

Sometimes the bell rang and they would force their way in to search the house. At that point, Marguerite, her daughter and I, and any other Jewish citizen that might be hiding in the attic, would climb out the skylight and lay silently on the roof of the four-story building until they went away.

Uncle was well known by the Germans for sabotaging their war efforts in World War I. In World War II, he was deeply involved in the underground. He had been denounced for hiding Jews in the rectory, and the Gestapo kept a vigilant eye on him. He would deny their accusations, and they would "promise" that they would get him another time. They were determined to catch him in the act.

The day after my arrival, I told Uncle Hubert that I wanted to join the Army of Liberation (AL) with its 7,000 active members. This was a section of the Belgian underground operating in Liège.

Uncle Hubert, 1914–1918. Picture given to me with his note on the back: "Have courage."

Uncle Hubert's rectory. On the top floor, near the third window on the left, we used to crawl out of the skylight and hide on the roof when the Germans came for inspection.

I needed a false ID. My present card showed me as a citizen of Montzen. I was supposed to be deported to Danzig, Germany. This ID would have me arrested immediately. I also needed a working card with a false name, address and place of birth. Uncle became visibly upset at the thought of my living such a dangerous existence. He went into a litany of warnings about the risks and dangers of such activities. "You are too young to do this type of work!" He argued that at seventeen, I would not be given the missions I felt would make a difference. He was so worried about my getting involved, but he knew that I was determined.

Within two days he handed me my first forged ID card and a sheet of counterfeit food stamps. With tears in his eyes he offered me a big hug, gave his blessing and bid me goodbye. He gave a firm warning of all the do's and don'ts, which I quickly tried to memorize, then sent me off to a family, (friends and patriots of the underground) to help in their household until my first assignment.

The false identification card, actually a false work card [Arbeitskarte]. The Germans treated it as identification, work for the war effort being their primary interest.

14 **Dangerous Rescue**
First Assignment with the Maquis (Resistance)

A visitor who pretended that he had an appointment with my uncle, Father Hubert, came into the kitchen where I was helping Marguerite. He said a password and pulled me into the small, dark, private dining room. Without introducing himself, he told me to leave within the hour and take the bus, if possible, back to the German border where I had just come from. "You will cross over the border on foot and stop at the farm near your Uncle Alphonse. You should look as though you are working there. Enter the farmhouse by the stable door. A young Jewish escapee from a Nazi holding camp will be waiting for you."

I found out much later, when my uncle was arrested for his activities in the Armée de la Libération and sent to this same camp, that the prisoners there were mostly Jewish people waiting to be shipped to Dachau.

The farm, modernized today, where I fetched Josh (X above the door.)

"You are to drill him until he knows his false ID by heart—new name, domicile and date of birth," said my commander. "Be sure he makes no mistakes! You will bring him back to Liège. Start at dusk so you will arrive in Liège late at night. Take him to your uncle-priest."

A friendly push to my shoulder, a hearty handshake, and then "Be careful! You'll be fine! God bless you!" was offered as his benediction. He went off with a fast, determined walk before I could utter another word.

Ouff, I thought to myself, as I quickly slipped the false ID into my bra. There was no time to give my orders a second thought. I ran upstairs to don my boots and some old dark clothes that would make me look like a farmhand. After a discreet hug from Marguerite and a short blessing from Uncle Hubert, I was on my way.

I knew that I had been assigned this mission because I could converse in German. People from Liège, the French-speaking part of Belgium, do not speak German and don't really want to learn it! Furthermore, the border-crossing near my home was well known to me. It was dangerous, especially for those carrying false IDs! I had to make the crossing twice—once to fetch the young man and once to bring him back.

My first border-crossing was successful. I met my Jewish contact at the designated farm in the late afternoon; he was a good-looking but very scared young man of about twenty-two. As we shook hands, I could feel a tremor in his frail, ice-cold hand. I presented him with his new ID and told him that he must commit it to memory in less than one hour. "We cannot leave here," I said, "until you know this and can respond to it even in your sleep."

Young people all over Belgium were being stopped at random by the Germans to show their IDs and prove that they were working. The German patrols would practically tear the card out of your hands and question you severely about its content. This was an intimidating tactic of theirs! It was absolutely imperative that my protégé be able to spit out that information accurately and assertively. A mistake would create immediate doubt and cost him arrest, prison, or even death.

Time was at a premium. We could not prolong our stay at the farm because the German border guards would stop there for a drink of milk or just to snoop around. Josh understood this without explanation. He was smart and anxious to leave that dangerous area on the border. My drilling session took less than half an hour. After that, I was unable to confuse him or trick him when questioned. Only once when I addressed him as "Josh" did he lift his head and respond, but from that mistaken moment on, only "Pierre" got his attention. I admired his quick mind and informed him that this would have to be the end of conversation between us. He was to follow— meticulously and without explanation—every order I gave.

Our awaited subtle knock came at the barn door. Uncle Alphonse, the gateman, came in. He had just closed the gates for a passing train. So we would not be frightened and think that a German guard was barging in, he whistled his familiar little tune on entering the stable. Sternly he ordered, "*Allez, ça y est, partez* [Move it, leave]!" with a sense of urgency, and ran back up to see the train passing.

We jumped up from our old three-footed milking stools, grabbed our coats, and quickly ventured down the dirt road in the opposite direction of the train crossing. We were able to pass the border without being detected.

Uncle Alphonse had danced around the area long enough to know exactly what to do to give us a safe passage. He had held up the border guards with his chatter, put down the gates long before the train arrived, and run through his house and down to the farm to warn us to leave as the train was passing. It was a long, slow merchandise train, giving us plenty of time to disappear, out of sight of the border patrols. Guards, guns and dogs were stuck on the opposite side of the track.

Dressed in rough working clothes and carrying a big walking stick that the farmer had provided, we climbed up onto the last field before the border. I reminded my young man not to utter a word, to keep his head down as though he were looking for mushrooms, and to just follow me. At one point I felt lucky to have nice, tall hedges to hide behind. Those were Belgian hedges, some as tall or taller than the farm buildings themselves. They protect the houses and farm dwellings from heavy snow and hard wind. They were a blessing to us as we traveled from one field to the next, helping us avoid any human contact on the roads. We were always fearful that the guards with their vicious German shepherds would detect us and send the dogs after us.

Suddenly, an unexpected noise stopped us in our tracks. My heart skipped a beat. *A dog,* I thought, as I conjured in my mind the things I would say if stopped. I expected a dog to pounce on us and listened for a

Cow in the meadow (likeness).

German shout of *Halt* or a shot, when slowly from around the tall hedge emerged the head of a cow. It was just curious and wanted to follow us. I tried to hush it and steer it away so it would not draw attention to us, but to no avail. Cows are really stupid!

In less than an hour we had crossed the border into old Belgium and the French-speaking section. I breathed a sigh of relief as I realized the gravity and danger of my mission. Bringing a Jewish escapee back over the border into safer territory was risking my life also!

At the end of this dirt road, there was a bus stop with a bus marked "Liège." I wanted to leap over and board it, but my cautious mind told me not to take the chance of being detected. Too many people were coming back from work, and Pierre and I still had a long way to go. I tried to be mindful of every detail, especially since my companion had a beautiful, dark complexion that made him look suspicious. Any German guard would have asked him for an ID. We continued on foot to the city of Herstal, where we dared to take a tram that would take us to Uncle's church.

The area that Josh/Pierre and I traveled to reach Liège.

Liège, at last! As usual, Uncle Hubert was in his study, no doubt praying for our safe arrival. Pierre, of whom I had grown quite fond, was sent to another residence; the rectory was not safe enough for him. He had a long way to go to get to Spain, Portugal and, eventually through the Channel to England. The Resistance would not take the chance of having him arrested at the rectory. He would be lodged with a much safer patriot and made ready for the next stretch of his journey.

Marguerite had again prepared a terrific hot meal for this tired, dirty, hungry pilgrim. Her hot bath and heavenly soothing foot massage following this feast seemed to make every pain and anxiety go away.

This sweet Jewish lady knew all about these kinds of trials. She and her daughter were now living at the rectory. In an effort to have them blend into his parish family, Uncle had enrolled the girl in Catholic school where she would, under false pretenses, make her first Communion with the rest of the children in her class.

Pierre was apparently getting the royal treatment in his one-night adoptive home. He would leave for Paris the next day. False French ID, a train ticket and French money had been orchestrated by the underground to send him to his next destination.

I was awarded a much-needed couple of hours of rest and spent the next day caring for my poor, blistered feet.

It was the night after our return when a message came from Colonel Prieux, a friend of my uncle's and a commander in the Resistance. In code, I was instructed to leave the area immediately and go to Banneux to the convent of the sisters of Saint Francis. The message had been sent to all people who had been instrumental in helping Pierre to escape.

Our young Jewish man, whom we had so painstakingly smuggled across the German border en route to London, had failed to follow orders. He had been instructed not to speak with anyone, not to trust anyone, not to go anywhere but to the designated places.

Temptation must have dictated his next move. He had arrived safely in Paris, but while transferring from the train to report to his next connection, he had stopped in a Paris café for a beer. Seated at the bar next to him were two innocent-looking men drinking a beer. Both wore civilian clothes and spoke fluent French. Little did he know that they were both Gestapos! Listening to everything our friend was discussing with the bartender gave them ample reason to question him, arrest him, torture him, and make him divulge some of the places and people who were instrumental in his escape.

A message sent to Uncle was a warning that the Gestapo would be arresting us by 5 a.m.

Pierre had been told no names or addresses of any one of us, nor specifics of Uncle's location. This made it impossible for the Gestapo to extract implicating information.

I fled to Banneux. My uncle was arrested and sent to prison for a few days, but they could prove nothing and released him, promising to get him the next time. I was unable to see him for a long time and then only if necessary and in a confessional.

My young protégé had robbed me of my security. Our nerves were severely shattered by his tragic outcome. We felt betrayed, discouraged and angry that this intelligent man had taken our collective efforts to save his life so casually. *Didn't he think of all of us who were now in such jeopardy? How could he have acted so irresponsibly?*

I spent a sleepless night worrying about my uncle and thinking of the torture and pain this poor young man would have to endure for daring to enjoy a moment of freedom.

* * * * *

Sanatorium run by Franciscan nuns to care for children with tuberculosis. After the war, the building was enlarged, named L'Hospitalité, and became a welcome place for pilgrims to Banneux. (story in chapter 15).

15 **False IDs to Banneux**

Can men really parachute from a glider and land in the middle of a large meadow near a castle without being detected? This was the question I asked myself when faced with one of my assignments.

That morning, Dr. L. had warned me to be ready to leave at a moment's notice. His home had become a *pied-à-terre*, an occasional hiding place when needed.

A total stranger, a man who looked like a *clochard* [hobo], arrived at the door. He was thin and tall and looked lost under his long, dirty black coat. As I walked in to meet him, I was struck by the sharp contrast of the luxurious studio where we were meeting, and the ghostly-looking figure who was pacing back and forth. He shook my hand, called me "Fernande," gave a password and, without further ado, explained the mission at hand. He was surprisingly well-spoken. He brought with him a small boy, about five or six years old, who looked pale and malnourished.

I never knew how or if the child knew the man in advance of this adventure, but the little fellow was not a bit mystified by the orders given to him. He understood that he was going on a trip to see a religious lady whom he knew and liked. She was working in the hospital where his doctor was sending him to get better. He seemed very happy with that idea.

While sending the youngster to the kitchen for a small snack, my mystery visitor gave me specific orders. "The boy will be your alibi," said he. "In reality, he will be admitted to the sanatorium of Banneux. If questioned about him, you are to explain that he is ill and that the sanatorium is his destination. Your work-card proves that you are an employee there."

From an old leather briefcase he pulled out a bundle of clothes belonging to the boy and wrapped them quickly in a red farmer's kerchief. From the inside pocket of his heavy coat came a small package the size of a deck of cards. It was wrapped in a shred of old, faded newspaper held together with a piece of raveled brown cord. He carefully placed the package in the middle of the bundle between the clothes and tightly closed it with a twist of the four corners of the kerchief.

The shrine of Banneux.

"The package inside," he explained, "contains life-saving items. Tonight, a group of English paratroopers are being flown in by glider to the meadows of the nearby castle. You are carrying the false identity cards for each one of these spies. Go to the sanatorium. Deliver the bundle to the Franciscan nun who runs the institution. Give the password. The sister is expecting you."

With a tight, strong handshake that expressed much more than words, he said, "Be careful! Good luck, and God be with you." Then my unknown compatriot disappeared.

I was struck by the strategy that was laid out for me, and especially by the importance of my mission. *I must not be caught! There is no margin of error! This mission cannot not fail!* I thought.

Totally focused on every detail given to me and planning every step to successfully achieve what was entrusted to me, I set out for Banneux with my little guest in tow.

I had gone there many times to pray at the Shrine of the Lady of the Poor, but never under such precarious circumstances. People come to Banneux on pilgrimage from all over Europe, to pray for sick or afflicted members of their families. Perhaps my guardian angel would help us get there safely! The little prayer that Maman had taught us as children came to my lips:

> *Ange de Dieu, qui êtes mon Gardien, par un bienfait de la Divine charité, éclairez-moi, protégez-moi et gouvernez-moi. Ainsi soit-il.*
> [Angel of God, who through God's goodness is my guardian, enlighten me, protect me, and guide me. Amen.]

The weather was unusually clear as we boarded the bus for an uneventful ride to Tancremont, about five kilometers from Banneux, our final destination. That part of the trip would have to be done on foot. The whole area of the shrine, sanatorium, convent and castle lent itself to clandestine activity and would surely be under scrutiny by the Germans. Walking this stretch demanded full concentration to the simplest detail. A shuffle of leaves in the woods or a rapid bird call to alert others could mean a villain was lying in wait.

The area at the edge of the Ardennes, a partly hilly section in southern Belgium and northeastern France, was lush with dense foliage, making a perfect hiding place. It held magnificent pine forests that were recommended for patients with tuberculosis, but it was also a truly peaceful and holy place where people came to pray and to find solace.

My charge and I walked hand in hand, almost silently. A sudden clearing through the trees along the road revealed a beautiful meadow up ahead. The sanatorium and the shrine were just around the corner and came into view after a sharp bend.

By now, my little guy showed serious signs of fatigue, and I was hoping and praying that I would not have to carry him. I started humming all the children's songs that he might know: *Au Clair de la lune; Savez-vous planter des choux; Meunier, tu dors.* He joined in and seemed to forget how sleepy he was.

I looked to the left of our bend. "Oh...there," I said, "we are almost there!"

"Oui, c'est ça [Yes, that's it]! exclaimed the little guy, with all the enthusiasm he had left.

Not a sound was heard, but we were in for the biggest shock of our lives. Within seconds, two members of the Gestapo (German State Police), stood in front of us. They had been waiting for us behind a mound of dirt piled up on the edge of a field. They wore long, gray-blue coats with what looked like a huge chain around their necks holding large metal letters, "GESTAPO," across their chests.

Two demons out of hell, I thought! They jumped out at gunpoint screaming *Halt!* and *Arbeitskarte* [Work-card]! at the top of their voices. At that moment, the last words of my dear father flashed through my mind: *Never show fear to your enemy. In your best German, speak louder than they do.*

I purposely took my time finding my false identity in the pocket of my work pants and handed it over to one of them.

"Where do you work?" he asked. We were in the French-speaking zone of Belgium, and he certainly expected that I would not understand his German question and would answer him in French. "Where do you work?" he repeated, a bit louder and more forcefully than before.

In the best German that I could muster, I boldly retorted, "Can you not read German? The answer is written on the card, in German." Then, lowering my voice I added, "I work over there," pointing to the tuberculosis sanatorium.

As instructed, I was carrying my red bundle on the end of a big stick, over my shoulder. "What is in the bundle?" he demanded, and "What is it with that kid?"

Again, I said loudly but calmly, "This child has tuberculosis. I am taking him to the sanatorium. In the bundle are his dirty clothes." While motioning that I was ready to slide the bundle off my shoulder, I inquired, "Do you wish to see them?"

At the sound of the word "tuberculosis," the macho Gestapo took a giant step backward and screamed, "*Raus! Raus! Schnell!* [Get out! Beat it! Fast!]" He was waving his arms nervously to send us away, while both of them retreated behind the pile of dirt, where I spotted their huge, shiny motorcycle. The thought of contamination had sent fear and panic into the Gestapos.

Our destination now in view, I took the hand of my crying child and resumed a normal pace. Those last few meters of our journey were the most difficult for me. I had felt strong during this threatening confrontation, but now, with our backs turned to them, danger seemed more imminent. *Would they change their minds and return for further inquiry? They were looking for something! Would they simply shoot us in the back?*

Suddenly, my legs felt like rubber, and I could feel the blood leave my head. I knew that I was white as a ghost. I felt a tremendous urge to get out of their sight but didn't dare run.

My strong faith in God came into mind. "Mary, mother of God," I said aloud, " I beg you, watch over your children. I need your help! Please, Lord, don't let me faint!"

My little "alibi" heard my ardent prayer and started to intone his own well-known prayer: "*Je vous salue Marie, pleine de grâce...*[Hail Mary, full of grace]," he began, and together we recited the entire prayer. He stopped crying; I was engulfed by a feeling of peace beyond understanding.

My firm belief in divine intervention never failed me. All I asked for was to be able to accomplish my mission, for God to let me reach my goal for the boys who would be arriving that night.

Thank God, we made it! Before I could put my hand on the bell of the cathedral-like entrance of the convent (photo, page 64), the door swung open. In the portal stood a Franciscan nun in her dark brown habit, arms outstretched like Jesus, to welcome us. "Come," said she, "I saw everything." Password given, she grabbed the precious bundle, opened a door, and handed it to an unseen accomplice. She rushed me into a small room and told me to recline for a short rest. Within a few minutes she brought me a mug of coffee, doused generously with the best cognac I have ever tasted. I have never forgotten the aroma and taste of her marvelous potion that seemed to cure my weary body instantly.

To my surprise, the sweet welcoming sister was German. She belonged to the German order of the Franciscans and worked as a nurse and a superior in this Belgian establishment. *A German nun, working and risking her life for the Belgian underground! May the Good Lord bless her!* I thought.

I would love to have stayed in that peaceful sanctuary for a while, but that was not part of the plan. I was to depart within half an hour. My little patient would happily stay with the nun, who turned out to be his aunt. I did not bid him *adieu*, nor give him another chance to see and recognize me. Such familiarity was not recommended!

My mission was accomplished, and my reward would be the spies landing successfully on the castle grounds that night.

* * * * *

16 **Raid on Liège**

Hitler was totally focused on winning the war. Around 1942, Belgians had endured another year of German occupation, deprived of their former lifestyle. The German economy was focused solely on manufacturing war equipment and making bullets. "Guns instead of butter" was Hitler's motto. Construction of bridges, highways and *autobahns* was in full swing, to facilitate rapid transport of troops, ammunition, trucks and tanks. Because of this, the German people had little or no access to luxury items. The occupying forces raided and depleted the Belgian stores of all goods that they could no longer buy at home. Fine lingerie, expensive clothing, and our world-renowned chocolate were popular items to send home. I remember that Maman could not keep a nice wool scarf or gloves for the winter on our store shelves. Our family store was virtually emptied of good quality merchandise.

Our beloved city of Liège was under siege. Every day was a new challenge! I never knew in which direction to go. Even going for a loaf of bread meant the possibility of being stopped and having to show my ID. We played the game of cat and mouse every time we stepped out of our home.

Place de la Liberté was a small city square, a popular place for young people to assemble and spend time with friends. There were exclusive boutiques all around the area. A place called Passage Lemonier had its entrance near the square. It was a much-frequented glass-covered promenade. People enjoyed strolling back and forth, admiring the most expensive clothes, the most stylish shoes, embroidered linens, or the gorgeous Belgian crystals of Val Saint-Lambert. We would spend hours window shopping and dreaming of the things we would never have.

I took a walk through this dreamy Galerie, up one side and down the other, stopping to stare at a beautiful dress in the window of a store I wouldn't dare to enter. I would have no need for such luxury, I was just happy to see it.

Right across the square was my favorite pastry shop. The square was unusually busy. Some young people were meandering, enjoying being with friends on a nice sunny day. Laughter and singing from one of the corners made us forget the tragedy of our present way of life.

As I left the Galerie, the upscale pastry shop with its fancy green awnings—my favorite spot—was calling me. I'd just take a look, as I usually did. I stood and stared for a while at small cream puffs and chocolate-dipped madeleines and éclairs. They were tantalizingly displayed in the window on gold leaf plates, waiting to be bought. *How was the baker able to get the scarce ingredients to make these goodies?* I thought to myself. Everything was rationed, and few people could afford to buy these delicacies. Perhaps the influx of Germans in the city of Liège allowed bakeries to buy more goods. Anything for the Werhmacht, you know!

As I stood there, a luscious chocolate-covered éclair seemed to stare at me, begging to be bought. I could not resist! No one was in the store but the baker himself, watching me out of the corner of his eye. An older man, he wore a white coat and an impressive white *toque* [baker's hat]. I had only small change, jingling in my pocket.

"Monsieur," I inquired timidly, "could you please tell me the price of an éclair?"

"Oui, Mademoiselle," he answered, "25 francs."

Hesitantly, I asked, "Would you be able to sell me half?" In Belgium, customers can buy an entire cake or just a slice of a delicacy.

"No," said the gentleman, in a tone of compassion, as I slowly put my few coins back in my pocket. "We cannot cut an éclair, Mademoiselle. The fresh cream would run out and it would not be sellable anymore."

Embarrassed, disappointed, and still hungry, I thanked the kind man, and headed for the door.

"Wait," I heard a voice saying from the rear. The baker, still behind the counter, was calling me back. He handed me the éclair, wrapped in a fancy paper boat. *"Voilà, ma petite,"* said he. "It is yours!"

"Oh no," I protested, fishing for the change from the bottom of my pocket. "I do not have enough money to pay for this éclair. I can't take this!"

By this time the man had rushed out from behind his fancy counter, put the precious treat in my hands, and said softly: *"Allez,* Mademoiselle, now you take this éclair and enjoy every morsel of it. I don't need money, and you need to eat this. You'll see how good it is. *Bon appétit !"*

I walked backwards toward the door and left my benefactor with sincere expressions of gratitude. I wondered how this man had known about my hunger. Could he tell from my pale face that this blessed éclair would be my first food of the day?

Out of the store, but still looking at him, I sunk my teeth into the luscious gift, and saw my baker waving, shaking his head and beaming with pleasure.

I slowly walked away, still savoring my treasure, and headed for the next corner to exit the square at one of its narrow streets. I had momentarily forgotten to keep up my guard. Suddenly, pandemonium broke out. There was instant panic!

Huge German military transport trucks parked crosswise on all roads leading out of the square and barred any vehicles from coming in or going out. They were closed in by khaki tarps that obscured their content. Within seconds German soldiers poured out of the trucks to stand guard on all sidewalks. They blocked every sidewalk leading out of the square. Minutes later, the backs of the trucks were opened and many more German patrols poured out.

They scuttled like rats into all the stores, including the Galerie, rounding up all young people sixteen to twenty years of age. Store exits in the back had guards stationed at every door. I saw no way to escape the kidnapping.

Hitler was now seeking Belgian youngsters from the French-speaking occupied part of Belgium, for his factories in Germany. They were being deported without notice.

The square, usually resounding with voices and laughter, was now filled with screams of fear and helplessness. Within a flash my brain was at war.

I was an underground agent with a false ID. I was an enemy of the Reich. Enemies of the Reich do not get deported; they get shot! My position was clear. I could not allow them to load me onto those trucks. I needed to get out of that square. It was my only option!

I swiftly walked up to the first narrow road leading out of the square, where two German guards held guns waist-high, pointed at each other to bar passage on the sidewalk.

Taking an instant to assess my predicament, I walked up lightheartedly to the younger-looking of the guards, put my hand on the barrel of his gun, looked flirtatiously into his eyes, and lifted the gun in the air to give myself space enough to crawl under. At the same time I was yelling in the best German I could muster: "You can't hold up a compatriot, my friend. I am running for my train to Aachen, where I work."

The soldier, who was not more than a youngster, was dumbfounded! In Liège, people don't speak German; it is purely French territory. As I was swirling myself out of this cursed trap, I heard him yell at his partner, who was probably aiming his rifle at me, "Don't shoot; she's German." He wanted to see my ID, but I was already out of range and on my way out of the square. Calling back to him I explained politely, "No time, but thank you, darling, I must catch my train!" Around the corner and into the alley I flew, thanking God once more for saving my life. This experience was totally unexpected and came as a real shock to me. I felt sick at heart for the parents and families of the poor kids who might never come back.

They would be waiting long into the night for a child who would not return.

The incident elicited more hate than ever for the occupying forces. From the lips of very angry people I heard expressions like *saligauds* and *les sales Boches*. Those were pejorative terms, the worst to describe human beings. If a German patrol were to hear you call one of them by those names, you would surely be arrested and severely punished.

* * * * *

17 **First Communion at Saint Bartholomew's**

On the festive day of First Holy Communion at Saint Bartholomew's, I ventured back to Liège, to my uncle's parish, to see Marguerite's young daughter participate in the service. Little Elise had been assigned a special teacher to learn the prayers and catechism required to practice the Catholic religion. Elise, a smart twelve-year-old Jewish girl, fully understood the importance of convincing everyone that she was a member of the Catholic faith. My uncle-priest, as Dean of the Catholic Church of Saint Bartholomew, was helping Elise and her mother to continue living incognito at the rectory.

The Church of Saint Bartholomew.

The big day had arrived! The clergy of the different parishes over which Uncle Hubert presided would attend. All of them had been incarcerated for their actions against the Reich, but were liberated by the Germans on May 23, to celebrate this important occasion in their respective churches.

People were astonished at this action, and viewed it as a gesture of good will on the part of the enemy. I found out later that the underground saw it as a ruse. It would give the Gestapo more exposure to Jews and their relatives who might be hiding in parishes. Some of those people in church were members of the Resistance, who were helping my uncle in this dangerous venture.

The sun was shining on the massive old Roman church. Banners were flying and the façade was adorned with wreaths of flowers. Church bells were ringing loudly, capturing the festive mood of the square as relatives and parishioners filed joyfully into the church. I slipped through the front portal, went immediately to the extreme right side of the nave, and sat in a pew, trying to protect my undercover profile.

I watched my uncle, who had also been released from jail for the big event. He was warmly welcoming the children, their parents, relatives, and all who came to celebrate the beautiful high mass.

The sound of the organ playing music of the old masters was exhilarating, and so was Uncle's resonant voice delivering prayers with fervor and reassurance. He knew his congregation and was well aware that more than one member of the underground was in church to pray with the families. Singing was intoned in traditional Latin and vernacular French. The packed church became alive, jubilant.

I will always remember Uncle Hubert slowly ascending the spiral stairs of the pulpit. Clad in his white and gold church robes, he stood on this magnificently sculptured platform, beneath an elaborately carved dome with a bright light beaming down on him. He looked like Moses preaching on the mountain.

He waited for total silence and the attention of his flock, then raised his arms toward heaven and delivered his well-prepared message to the people. His homilies were always uplifting and reassuring masterpieces, and this one was no exception. His resounding voice rang in my ears for days afterward.

During this solemn celebration, and then only for a the moment, people forgot the fear, hunger and pain of their miserable existence. This was a big day in their children's lives. The congregation was now totally focused on remembering the words of Jesus at the Last Supper, which we believe were meant not only for his Apostles, but for us, his followers: "This is my body, this is my blood, the blood of the New and everlasting Covenant. Do this in memory of me." Catholics believe that the bread and wine are transformed into the body and blood of Christ in the Eucharist. For the first time in their lives, the children would obey the Lord's command and receive the consecrated body and blood of Christ.

The children all rose from their seats, hands folded in prayer, and processed slowly, one by one, up toward the altar where the priest would place a small white wafer on their little tongues, saying, "The Body of Christ." Then they bowed their heads and returned quietly to their seats. They knew to thank God for the gift of love that they had received in the consecrated host.

Little Elise had learned her lessons well and felt quite comfortable participating in the ceremony. To honor her religious beliefs, Uncle Hubert offered her un-consecrated bread. She was aware of the procedure and was agreeable to that.

When the Mass ended, the church bells again rang out joyfully. The girls, decked out in their short white dresses, and the boys in their jackets, short pants, and bow ties, hands folded in prayer, looked angelic as they silently processed out of the church under the proud, watchful eyes of their parents and the congregation.

Father Hubert followed them, stopping here and there to greet and congratulate parents.

A sudden change of mood was felt in the exiting congregation. I turned to face the children, glanced at the back doors of the church, and was shocked by what I saw. Two fully uniformed Gestapos stood at attention inside the portal, one on the right, the other on the left. They said nothing, just scrutinized every child and adult with affront. I could only imagine the feelings of the children, forced to exit the church between these two threatening soldiers. And what about Elise? I could not see her face, but knew that she must have panicked at the sight of them. She had played her part well during the mass, and no one could have detected that she was not Catholic. I felt sorry and scared, and quickly called on my guardian angel to come to her protection.

The short-lived peace ended with the parents rushing to get out of the church to protect their children from fear or harm.

I understood immediately why my uncle had not acknowledged me with a look or a nod when he was leaving the church and passed by my pew. In those days, the priest celebrated mass from behind the altar, facing the people, so he had observed the unwelcome guests during the entire mass. On the other hand, the parishioners faced forward and did not know that the Germans were there until they turned around to leave the church.

I wondered: *Did the soldiers understand and would they heed the message of love and compassion in my uncle's homily?*

Their presence totally distracted me. *Why were the Gestapo here in our church? Which one of us were they looking for?*

When Uncle Hubert left the church behind the children, the Gestapo followed, but did not speak to him. *Would they dare arrest him in front of the children, in front of his church, after such a Holy Mass? What an insult to Belgian Catholics!* These thoughts raced through my mind as I stayed a few minutes, planning my next move.

Uncle Hubert soon came walking back into the church, passed my pew and whispered, "*Ça va, ils sont partis* [It's okay, they have left]!" I slipped out immediately and vanished into the city.

I would have loved to spend a few minutes at the rectory, maybe sharing a meal with Uncle, but the sad reality was that my next encounter with this dear man would be in the confessional. To return to the rectory had become far too dangerous.

I would go at scheduled confession hours, check that no suspicious people were watching, and quickly kneel in one of the two small booths to speak to my uncle. He would open the small wooden window that separates priest from penitent, and we would briefly exchange messages or important information.

During one such encounter, my uncle admitted that he had never prayed so hard for God to come down Himself to protect the children, as during the First Communion ceremony. He had known of the presence of the two Gestapos in church from the very beginning of the service. I marveled at his faith, his stamina and his composure.

This episode is a reminder of the tragedies endured by nuns and priests working undercover to help other human beings. Montzen will never live down the arrest and decapitation of their beloved young Vicar, Father Jean Arnolds. He came to Montzen in 1940 and worked furiously to save the children from Hitler's godless system of education that was corrupting the minds of our youths. He was arrested and decapitated for hiding Allied flyers and helping the Resistance with the Jewish escapees.

His father was also arrested for the same reasons, and died in a concentration camp.

Saintly men they were! They shall never be forgotten.

Father Jean Arnolds

18 **My Family at Home during the War**
Cows for the Wehrmacht

I was away from Montzen for most of the war, and I missed the companionship of my brothers and sisters. I often yearned for their support in the life and death situations that I was going through alone. At least, they had each other to share the pain of their trials.

At home, my parents lived a nerve-racking existence: watching, listening, and striving to rear their children while obeying the rules and regulations imposed by the Germans. Unrest in the area had been prevalent for a long time. Even before the invasion, people were conditioned to run for their lives at the least warning. It had already begun in 1939 when, one Sunday afternoon, Montzen Gare was invaded by a crowd of refugees coming from Gemmenich, the village next to us, but right on the border of Germany. There had been an alert about an expected invasion. People claimed that they heard heavy equipment and motor vehicles being moved closer to the Belgian border. They heard before they saw! They were living in the shadow of Hitler's army! They needed no more evidence. Panic struck the town. "The Germans are coming! The Germans are coming!" was the cry. People migrated to Montzen to get on a train and run for their lives. This incident was repeated several times early in 1940, before the actual invasion took place.

Montzen Gare had threats of its own. The nightmare of a surprise Allied bombing was always present. "Be ready and be vigilant" was Papa's motto.

Surprisingly, even in wartime, my family's sense of humor sustained them. When I returned home after the war was over, they had many stories to share. My sister Mary and brother Joseph told the story of what happened in the field between the station and our house the day before the bombardment of Montzen

Gare. Recounting it, even years later, still brought tears of laughter to their eyes.

Angry farmers delivered their cows that had been requisitioned by the enemy; many chose old animals that were no longer producing a lot of milk. The Germans were now confiscating some of their milk supply as well! Mary compared the field to a medieval market place. The onlooking villagers were told by the farmers to go ahead and milk the cows before the Germans loaded them on the trains to be shipped to Germany.

Mary said that is was so comical to see people running every which way for buckets. "*What were they going to do with so many buckets of fresh milk?*" she wondered. But it didn't matter: "That much less milk for *les Boches!*" It was a matter of revenge, claiming that which was theirs!

Late into the day, hundreds of cows were mooing in the field while the heartbroken farmers watched their livestock being loaded onto an immense train and shipped over the viaduct to the Reich. By handing over their cows, the farmers rightly felt they were contributing to the well-being of the enemy. A bitter thought indeed!

Another moment of humor came when a farmer had his horses in hiding. Oh yes, "in hiding"! When it came to livestock, Hitler was avaricious. He needed them! He was requisitioning livestock of all kinds, especially horses. Farmers were even fearful of taking them to market or using them to deliver cows to the station. The Germans would requisition the horses on the spot.

Always ingenious, the farmers found new ways to disguise and hide the animals before the Wehrmacht took them, either to slaughter the weak and the old, or to draft the strong and hardy into their cavalry.

We all had a good laugh when my brothers told the story of a farmer who hurriedly pushed the horse into one of the stalls before the German inspectors arrived, covered the animal's face and body with a brown cloth, and then filled the stall with hay that covered the entire animal up over the top of his head. The owner hoped and prayed that the horse would not neigh during the inspection.

The family loved telling stories of their little victories over the aggressors in their life of oppression and tyranny. No one lived a normal life.

Yet, within twenty-four hours Montzen Gare would witness another, far different scenario.

* * * * *

Papa and my oldest brother Joseph were convinced long ago that our railroad station would be attacked sooner or later. All of Montzen knew it would happen; it was just a matter of time.

German aviation controlled the airways. By 1943, however, air superiority had shifted to the Allies, especially the American Air Force. They were attacking German war factories and ammunition depots almost nightly, and on a large scale. This was a crushing assault on the enemy.

Joseph and Papa decided to build a safe place for the family. They chose our garage, which housed a small truck used to deliver groceries to customers. The second floor was Papa's studio/workshop where, as a child, I would join my father to work on special projects, like building the frame for our gazebo or repairing a piece of furniture. Sandbags were brought in to line the four inside walls of the garage. Huge beams were hoisted against the first floor ceiling for support. Sandbags would cover the entire second floor above. The new bunker was well-equipped with tools to shovel oneself out, medical supplies to take care of injuries, and food and water for a few days.

Once the serious attacks began, Papa and Joseph took turns staying up all night listening to the *verboten* [forbidden] BBC and the German *Luftlagen-meldung.* Both radio stations announced enemy planes advancing over the Channel and told the direction in which they were flying. If necessary, Papa or Joseph—whoever was on duty—would alert the family. Orders from Papa were to grab shoes and a coat and run for the bunker. All of them went to bed partially dressed, just in case. They also were to make sure that every brother and sister was accounted for.

Then came the fateful night of April 28, 1944, the bombardment of Montzen Gare! Although I was not there, my family still talks about that horrendous night.

Joseph was on duty, listening to the radio. Around 1 a.m., he heard warnings on the German radio station announcing enemy bombardiers approaching the Belgian coast and heading for Aachen. Hurriedly, he alerted the family, who had been sound asleep. Sirens were screaming through the darkness! By the time they all grabbed their shoes and coats, rushed down the stairs, out the door and into the bunker, flares had already lit up the skies. Papa said: "It was like daylight over the entire region."

Once in the bunker, everyone sat on a wooden bench, frozen in fear, with their backs pressed against the heavy beams to shore up the walls. The bombs were dropping at rapid intervals. Six at a time they fell, shaking the bunker and making the beams sway a bit from side to side.

"We could hear pieces of our roof and all sorts of stuff flying overhead," said Cecile. "We were choking on the dust that filled the bunker." Screams pierced the darkness as homes and buildings were being smashed into thousands of pieces.

I asked if anyone was crying, and what Maman was doing during this horrible time. The answer came quickly from my youngest sister: "The more bombs that fell, the louder Maman and all of us prayed, *Herr hilf uns, wir gehen zu Grunde* [Lord help us! We are going under]! There was no time for long prayers, only supplication, a reminder of the fragility of our situation. The pause between bombs was excruciating. According to my poor little sister, "We simply died with fear, thinking *maybe the next one will get us!*"

Maman, whose first name was Josephine, loved her patron saint. She had brought her ten-inch statue of Saint Joseph with her into the bunker, and had placed it in a corner on one of the heavy supporting beams, pleading with God to protect her family. At the end of the bombardment, the statue of Saint Joseph was still there, on the beam in the bunker. It never fell off, never moved!

The village chapel, about 500 meters behind our house, had been flattened, as were the homes of three neighbors and many other dwellings including the Belderbusch castle.

This was the Allied attack on Montzen Gare that Papa had expected and prepared for! My parents called it "a moment in the Underworld."

Planes had showered the area with flares. A hundred and twenty aircraft heavy bombardiers flew in formation. Twelve hundred heavy-caliber bombs with late detonators and countless incendiary bombs were dropped from their cargo holds. All fell on the station and the surrounding area in less than half an hour. The results of the attack were devastating. That section of Montzen counted 65 deaths, 10 persons unaccounted for, and 150 persons wounded. Fifty-seven houses were totally destroyed, 71 were gravely damaged, and 410 people were left homeless.

The railroad yard and station were totally destroyed. The aftermath will never be forgotten. School did not reopen until the war had ended.

Destruction of Montzen Gare (1).
(from the uncredited booklet *Montzen-Gare se souvient [Montzen-Gare remembers]* ! ca. 1985)

Destruction of Montzen Gare (2) and a bomb crater.
(from the uncredited booklet *Montzen-Gare se souvient [Montzen-Gare remembers]* ! ca. 1985)

The Allied bombing of Montzen Gare had left our house still standing but uninhabitable! There were broken windows, loosened stairs, and a roof almost gone. To top it off, the foundation had moved ten centimeters from under the house. After inspection by German engineers, no one was allowed inside the building; it was condemned. Miraculously, the bombing had left our family intact with no injuries. Papa's bunker had rocked and swayed, but it had held up and saved our family. Maman claimed that it was Saint Joseph who had protected them all.

When the bombing ended, Papa and Joseph rushed out with pick and shovel to rescue our next door neighbor, who could be heard through the cellar window crying for help. As they dug frantically to get him out from under the crushed house, Papa could see his hand at the basement window and told his dying neighbor that they would get him out of there. His wife and child died when heavy cement beams crushed their bodies. Other neighbors came to help, but it was in vain! The weight of the debris that had fallen on top of them had taken its toll. Hubert Laixhay expired before people could reach him.

Papa was in tears when he recounted the tragedy to me. He had been unable to rescue his good neighbor and said sadly: "We couldn't do it, we couldn't get to him fast enough. He didn't listen to my warnings to prepare for that fatal day."

Before moving on to the next house to help another family, Papa gave permission to Maman and the children to leave the bunker. Cecile and Hubert tell how they found our yard in the dark of night. "Only a gleam of light from a burning fuel tank in the bombarded railroad yard helped us to climb out over the debris. Our garden was pocketed with huge craters from the fallen bombs," Cecile said. "We just stood there, paralyzed. We couldn't move, couldn't cry. We just stood there in shock.

"We climbed over the craters, the debris, the piles of glass, and ventured into our house, which was still standing. There," said Cecile, "in disbelief, we found ourselves facing the large *papier-mâché* statue of Saint Joseph that belonged in the Chapel where it had stood on a pedestal for many years. The Chapel was totally flattened. Yet there it was, sitting in our house, unharmed!"

As I have said, Maman had always had a great devotion to Saint Joseph, the patron saint of families. At the end of daily prayers, she would implore him to protect her family and grant us all a peaceful death. Cecile said, "We never understood how the Chapel statue could have been blown through the air and landed in our house without a scratch." Maman needed no explanation; she just stood there holding her ten-inch statue from the bunker in her hand, looking in awe at the larger one from the chapel standing in her house. She was convinced that Saint Joseph had kept her family under his loving protection.

After making sure that our family was safely out of the bunker, Papa and Joseph grabbed some heavy tools and went to the next house, which was also destroyed. There the entire family was alive in the cellar, screaming for help through the half-moon hole between the first and second step at the door of the house. This hole was used to receive a truckload of coal or a supply of potatoes for the winter. The delivery man would place a chute from the back of his truck to the opening, and deliver merchandise right into the cellar.

Papa decided that since the house was totally flattened, all they could do to save their neighbors was to clear away the fallen bricks and the mound of debris, make the hole larger by removing the two front stone steps, and bring the people out that way. Help came from neighboring villages, and that entire family was brought out, one by one, from what could have been their grave.

Château Belderbusch (XVIth century) before the bombings.
(From the uncredited booklet *Montzen-Gare se souvient [Montzen-Gare remembers]* ! ca. 1985)

Nearby Château Belderbusch was totally destroyed. During the heavy bombing, the moat around the castle gave way and the canalization broke. The entire family drowned in the cellar where they had taken refuge.

Château Belderbusch after the bombardments. (From the uncredited booklet *Montzen-Gare se souvient [Montzen-Gare remembers]* ! ca. 1985)

My brother Hubert tells another story of that fatal night when Papa and Joseph had already pulled an entire family out of the cellar. A priest from the adjacent village came to help; it was Father Schmets. He had set out on his bicycle, without light, in the middle of the night, to assist the wounded and the dying. The priest was offering prayers, administering Holy Communion and giving the last rites to the dying, when the

German Todt rescue squad arrived. They were a group of very young German men who were sent to the areas where disaster had struck. Their task was to move people out of danger or get them to the hospital. When they saw the priest, they treated him like a charlatan and tried to chase him. "We don't need your foolish talk or your services here," they said, and threatened to kill him if he continued. The Belgian people were enraged at their arrogance. Without a moment's hesitation, the Belgian men formed a tight circle around the wounded and dead lying on the ground, and called Father Schmets into the circle, asking him to continue his services. They stood, hats off, in prayer with the priest, then turned facing the Germans and threatened to kill them if they dared to interfere.

A German law said that, in cases like this, the military was to back off and withhold all retaliation. It forbade its troops from reacting with violence in the wake of disaster. It was the only time that Belgian people could blatantly insult invading troops without being severely punished. The idea was to let the protest be expressed and avoid adding insult to injury or risk a riot.

Todt retreated in the face of insults and threats. Hubert said that the Belgian people would definitely have carried out their threats to kill any German who tried to stop the priest.

Montzen Gare had had its final blow while Montzen Village, just a twenty-five minute walk from our home, had been left almost intact.

I had been told about this huge bombardment by the Resistance and was informed that my family was alive. With Montzen Gare in rubble, and no home to stay in, my brothers and sisters were farmed out with different relatives. My parents began the task of finding a small place for the ten of us to live together; they were anxious to reunite their family.

My brother tells of all kinds of evil-doing that had taken place at the railroad station and in the village prior to the bombardment. Life in Montzen Gare had gone from bad to worse. People had gotten used to the occupying enemy, and there was a sense of tolerance that made life livable even though anger and antagonism were always present.

He told a story of sabotage on a high scale. Once a Belgian railroad employee put a trainload of stolen French Limoges china, headed for Germany, onto the wrong rail. The three loaded cars went crashing into a cement wall that was used to stop trains if they lost their brakes and were out of control. Not a single piece of china was saved to make its way to Germany.

Another incident brought delight and laughter to the whole village. Tankers, loaded with French wine ready to go over the viaduct and into Germany, were sabotaged. Word got around that wine was flowing onto the tracks. The villagers ran with buckets to collect the delightful drink that was pouring out like a spigot from the perforated tank.

Another time, the German school teacher, hired by the occupying government to replace our homegrown ones, insisted on reciting a German poem and singing a German song to start each day. This was instead of saying a prayer and singing our Belgian national anthem.

In my brother's class, where pictures of the Belgian king and all religious crosses had been removed, students were to face the picture of Hitler that had been mounted over the teacher's desk, and sing. The teacher would start, but when it was time for the children to join in, there would be silence. Absolute silence! The teacher punished the students by not allowing them to go to lunch until they complied. By 1:30 p.m. the German teacher was so hungry and frustrated that he dismissed them all.

November 11, Armistice Day, had always been reverently celebrated in Belgium to honor the fallen men of World War I. Fathers of the school children made small Belgian flags for the boys' lapels, and they were handed out within view of the school. All students wore them proudly and defiantly. When the teacher came in with the greeting of "Heil Hitler," there was no response. "All students wearing the flag, stand," said the teacher. The entire class stood up, straight and proud. The police were called in. By the time the chief arrived, the children had removed all their flags. The chief of police, in full uniform, tried to intimidate them with, "All students who had worn the flag, stand." The entire class stood up again with gusto.

The chief was shocked by the children's fearless attitude. He told them to tell their parents, both mothers and fathers, to report to the police station the next morning at 9 a.m. Then he told the children to stand and salute him with "Heil Hitler" before going home. The class quietly rose and silently made the sign of the cross.

The next morning all the fathers reported as ordered, but the mothers stayed home. The police hall could not hold all of them, but the chief still proceeded to give the fathers a lecture on how children should behave in their classes. Some of the men started to ask stupid and totally irrelevant questions, wasting time and making a mockery of the meeting. Belgians in that part of the country had learned German in school and were less fearful of the authorities. They could communicate comfortably with them in their language.

The chief became angry and intimidated and called off the meeting. The people had won a small victory once more.

Sabotage had become a way of life for the children as well as for their parents.

* * * * *

By 1943, the underground lines of information were in full swing and were a great help to the Allies. There was heavy bombing by the Allied forces over Germany. Ammunition installations, as well as any organization helping Hitler in his war effort, were being destroyed.

Parents of young people eighteen or older, who had been deported to work in factories in Germany that might be targeted, lived in a state of constant anxiety.

Frequently, during the day, air raid sirens went off. All traffic stopped and people ran to the shelters, hoping that they were not near a railway junction or a target that had been marked for destruction. If a target was missed, we knew that the bombers would be back again to finish the job. The heavy roaring of the bombardier squadrons flying over the Channel, heading toward Belgium, was heard long before the planes were seen advancing in a bird-like V-formation.

What a feeling! The first reaction is fear, then one instinctively looks for the nearest shelter! Sixty years later, that feeling still haunts me. I was badly marked by that sound. One day, when I was teaching one of my first classes at Germantown Academy in Fort Washington, Pennsylvania, I heard a low-flying aircraft, which I took for a loaded plane, coming from the nearby air base and advancing over our school. It made the windows rattle. I instantly glanced at the long oval table I would have to push against the windows, and tell my kids to get under, to be protected from flying glass or shrapnel. In a flash, my mind had returned to war.

German anti-aircraft would be blasting away at the American convoy, bringing down as many planes as possible. Belgian patriots would race out to get to the crash before the Germans, and retrieve the fallen airmen. The rescuers would hand them over to the

Resistance for protection from the horrors of prison camp, or execution.

Assisted by Belgian doctors and members of the Resistance, the servicemen would hopefully be repatriated via several clandestine lines organized by the Belgian and French underground. Some downed airmen wandered away from their crash site and hid in the forest, until they felt that it was safe to come out and look for help. Occasionally, imposters were found among them, so strict guidelines were established for thorough interrogation to make sure that those who were being rescued were genuine Allied airmen in need of help, rather than Germans dressed in American or English uniforms.

We were told that Americans of German descent left the U.S. around 1941 and came back home to fight the war on the German side. They knew the American way of life, spoke perfect English, and became prize recruits for the German army, to spy on

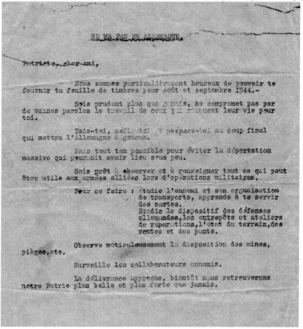

Clandestine letter of warning to Resistance workers (translation, p. 99).

underground activities. The Belgians (non-declared foot soldiers), would swiftly do away with such traitors. The danger that such an individual could inflict on the clandestine functioning of the underground was tremendous. We knew only too well that we could not endanger the lives of the many brave patriots committed to returning the airmen safely to England.

Translation of letter of warning, hand delivered to me in July 1944, only days before the arrival of Americans in Liege.

Do Not Go to Germany

Patriot, dear friend:

We are particularly happy to be able to send you food stamps for August and September '44.

Be careful more than ever--don't compromise by vain words, the work of those who risk their lives for you. Be silent! Do not talk! Prepare for the final blow which will put Germany on its knees.

Do all you can to avoid the massive deportation that could take place soon.

Be ready to observe and report all that can be useful to the Allied forces during their military operations.
For this you must:
    Study the enemy and his organization of transport, learn to use maps;
    Study the disposition of German defenses, military depots, repair workshops, the state of their campaign grounds and of the roads and bridges;
    Observe meticulously the disposition of mines, traps, etc.;
    Keep an eye on enemy collaborators.

Deliverance is approaching; we will soon find our nation more beautiful and stronger than ever.

A complicating factor was the growing Rexist movement on the outskirts of Brussels. This was a Belgian pro-Nazi party, which was considered the scum of the earth. They were dangerous because they would report any suspicious activity to the German authorities.

With the Rexists in mind, the Resistance was always on the lookout for safe houses where airmen could be concealed. They needed provisions and protection until they could be flown back to England. During my years as an operative in this organization, I delivered many forged food stamps, ID cards and messages, always well aware of the fierce consequences if caught by the Gestapo. The tragedy of a Belgian and French group of citizens who were condemned to death and faced a German firing squad was well publicized in the newspapers. Anyone who dared to give help of any kind to fallen airmen, or failed to report their whereabouts to the German headquarters, could count on the swift hand of the German War tribunal. The penalty of death was enforced without pity.

By 1944, we felt that the end of the war was near, but life had become even more precarious. The Germans, who were losing ground, grew nastier, and sabotage escalated; they continued arresting and deporting trainloads of patriots as enemies of the Reich. Flyers were sent out to members of the AL (Army of Liberation) urging us to report anything from the location of stored ammunition, the placement of anti-aircraft guns, a pontoon bridge thrown over the Meuse river, sightings of trains of petrol heading to France. All of these were of interest to the Allies across the Channel.

We led a life of fear, skepticism, anger, excitement, and caution—always caution. Every step I took, every door I entered, every person I met, every waking moment, held the possibility of adventure or tragedy.

Once I was on a tram in Liège to deliver a false ID card. I had it hidden in my bra, as usual. Suddenly German guards stopped the tram. Passengers were told to get off while authorities conducted a search. IDs were examined as we boarded again. I was pulling my sweater together over my bosom when a tall, stocky older gentleman noticed that I was trying to hide something. He skillfully slid in front of me and partially hid me from the Germans as he fumbled in his coat for his own ID. With his help I was able to show my ID and slip by the German guard without being questioned.

A sign of gratitude was certainly in order, but this would have violated our discretionary methods. This seemingly kind soul could have been a Rexist, a member of the *maquis* (the underground Resistance movement), or simply the minister of the local church. For good reason, "trust no one" was our motto! Contrary to my nature, I managed an indifferent smile and thanked God for the man's help.

German patrols were everywhere. We lived in constant fear, yet people invented creative new ways to annoy the occupying enemy wherever possible.

When the Germans didn't like the way they were harassed by the public, their *Kommandantur* [Command Post] would issue new laws against the offenses. I was always amused at their frustration.

People would smoke on trains, trams, and in public places, and purposely burn holes in the uniforms of German soldiers standing close by. As I said, I was amused by such antics, but the German *Kommandantur* was not! Their humorless response was to issue a new law: no more smoking on trains or trams.

What the Germans did not know was that Belgians were experts at circumventing a law they did not like.

I never saw it done, but my oldest sister Bertha— who by this time had been drafted to repair damaged German uniforms—told me that on the city trams people were using some kind of acid to burn holes in the heavy winter coats of the occupying forces standing nearby.

Belgians were never stopped by edicts from the *Kommandantur*. They made it a sport to get around those laws. People would risk any kind of punishment to make a statement.

Our hearts were heavy and nerves were shattered, but hope was in the air. Our American deliverers were near, and we knew that with God's help, they would help us regain our freedom.

* * * * *

22 **Return to Montzen**

I was in Andenne with Madeleine D. when we heard that the American troops were heading north toward Huy, Liège and the German border. Returning home to see my family and to witness the disaster was now a possibility.

The Americans had arrived! What a sight! What jubilation! People of all ages were running to the center of Andenne to see the long-awaited troops from the United States of America rolling up Main Street, heading to the front.

Church bells were ringing nonstop! People lined the streets and barely let the convoy advance. When they stopped, even for a brief moment, girls would climb up on those huge tanks to hug and kiss our liberators. In the face of each brave man, we saw our freedom. There were screams of joy, but also tears of sadness from families who had either lost a son in the war or whose loved ones were still in German prison camps, behind enemy lines. There was no certainty that they would all return safely.

I watched the most impressive column of military equipment, which looked like monsters rolling by. My sister used to stand and count the wheels of their trucks. Eighteen-wheelers! I had never seen such awesome machines; just to look at them gave us an overwhelming feeling of power and hope. Real monsters on our little Belgian highways! There was no doubt of victory.

For the first time I slipped on my newly issued "Resistance" armband. Using the few words of English that I had made part of my vocabulary, I was able to convince a tall African-American truck driver and his companion to give me a ride to the city of Huy, about fifteen kilometers away. I had been told by a member of the military police that the American headquarters was in Huy, and I was looking for a way home to Montzen to be with my family. They would be facing the battle at the front line when the American troops arrived.

My plea for a ride must have been convincing, for when the order came to move on, I suddenly felt an arm around me. The playful driver's companion saw that I could not reach the running board of the truck, so he hoisted me by my waist into the cab of their gigantic ammunition truck. They gave me the ride of my life, all the way to Huy in this endless military convoy. I had not given much thought to the possibility that we might be bombed. I was too intent on sprinting for home to arrive in Montzen with the liberators.

Having been through an interrogation (to verify the legitimacy of my request) at the U.S. headquarters in Huy, I finally was taken to the commander, who showed me a big map of Belgium hanging behind his desk. All I wanted to know was the direction I should travel to avoid capture by the Germans.

The dear man pointed out on his map that my hometown and surrounding villages were not totally liberated and that the Americans were barely in Aachen. Pockets of German troops were still reported fighting in the countryside. "If you go," he said in a rather authoritative voice, "I cannot be responsible for your safety."

This gentleman reminded me of my father. I thanked him respectfully and told him that I had not seen my family for years. I had to go. He frowned at me, with the same look of disapproval I'd seen on my Papa's face when I was stubborn. I felt dismissed without help or permission to go.

On my way out, I thanked him again, and I saluted him as a soldier would. As I started walking toward the door, I heard a voice calling me back, in good French. "Wait," he said, "*Je vous donne un coup de main* [I'll give you a hand]."

He called in two infantry soldiers, armed with machine guns, and ordered them to take me home to Montzen! Yes, all the way to Montzen! I tried to tell him that this was not necessary, but my gentle commander was suddenly taking charge. All I could do was follow orders.

In a flash we were rolling toward Liège and heading for Montzen in a jeep. I was escorted by a driver and the two soldiers with their guns pointed to the outside. One was in the passenger seat and the other was on my left in the back seat.

As we approached the area near Montzen and the German border, we encountered gunfire from some German troops hiding in the fields. The two GIs in my jeep reacted instantly. Bullets were flying! The one sitting at my left grabbed me by the neck, and pushed me down to the floor, while the driver kept on speeding ahead until he found my family. It was a short but frightening confrontation!

After the attack, my protective GI apologized for having treated me so roughly to save me from the bullets. We arrived in Pannesheydt, the village adjacent to Montzen, and found my family still hiding in the cellar of their small, temporary abode.

I knocked at the little cellar window above the ground and could hear Papa's voice. It rings in my ears today. "*Mon Dieu*, [My God] there is Fernande!" My heart leaped, for it had been two and a half years since I had heard that loving voice.

The front door of the little stone house flew open. There stood Papa and Maman, open-armed and in tears! After enthusiastic embraces from Maman, Papa, and all my brothers and sisters, the love and the warmth of "home" engulfed my whole being. I was in heaven!

We turned to thank my benefactors, who had risked their lives to help me find my people, but their only concern was that we all return to the cellar. One of them knew the French word for cellar and kept calling *"cave, cave,"* pointing to the cellar, as they quickly disappeared.

That night we prayed for them and for our gift of life.

* * * * *

23 The Miracle of the Piano
My life in Liège under German attacks

After the family recovered somewhat from the shock
of seeing me alive and home, I went back to Liège
to help Uncle Hubert and earn some money to help
sustain the family. The Germans were still attacking
Americans on Belgian soil. We were now coping with a
miserable existence of another kind. My life was so
different from that of the rest of my family. The war
was still raging. I worried about them and asked God
to protect and keep them alive. At least, they had a
place to call home and a pillow for their heads at
night.

I was mostly on my own, with a very busy uncle,
often lonely and scared. The bombing had increased
dangerously over the city, and involvement in rescue
operations was frequent. Once, I was ready to leave
our doctor's house when alarms signaled another
bomb. As I helped push his children down the cellar
stairs, a bomb came whistling down, hitting the
houses across the narrow street and removing the
façade of every house in the row. People fell from the
second and third floors of their houses onto the street,
and to an untimely death. It was a dreadful tableau.

My guardian angel had saved me once again! I
tried to rise from my crouched position at the top of
the stairs. My head and shoulders were wearing the
cut-glass transom window that had adorned the top of
the front door. Broken glass was all over my body and
in my hair. I must have looked pretty sad in my
button-less winter coat. The buttons had been ripped
off by the blast of air or by shards of glass that flew in
every direction. The beautiful beige wool coat that my
sister Bertha had painstakingly tailored for me looked
like a bloody rag.

While my family endured the attack on our village,
I had my own experiences with Hitler's bombs. He
sent deadly "buzz-bombs" as we called them, or more
specifically, the V1 jet-propelled bombs, (a pilot-less

airplane), and the V2 German rocket-propelled bombs, against England. It's been said that at the height of their trajectory, these bombs reached the stratosphere and attained a speed greater than the speed of sound.

All I can say is that when the frightening sound of these deadly birds was heard, we stopped dead in our tracks and listened. If the motor stopped, we only had time to run for cover, any place that shielded us from broken glass hurled at us at high speed by an exploding bomb.

Once, I was on the second floor in the rectory of Uncle's church, when I heard a plane flying toward Liège. I quickly opened the window and clearly saw a bomb passing over us, continuing toward the Channel. Or so I thought! Suddenly, the sound stopped, then the horrible whistling noise that announced death and destruction fell on the other side of Liège. Sometimes these bombs would travel in one direction, leading us to mistakenly think we were safe, then suddenly make a half-moon turn and come back and hit nearby. When they passed overhead, I'd listen to their roar and learned to evaluate where they were heading. I'd look for the long tail of fire to see what direction it was taking. If the motor stopped before I could see it, I knew that I was probably the target and, like an animal pursued by a hunter, ran for my life.

People in Liège had a hard time believing that all these "vengeance weapons," or *vergeltungswaffen*, as the Germans called them, were destined for England. Too many ended up on Liège and Antwerp. Too often, I was surrounded by cries and screams and had to help remove dead victims from cellars and houses that had near direct hits. People were convinced that Hitler meant to hit Liège, that it was not by mistake.

I cannot recall the exact number of bombs Liège took on a single day, but I think it was somewhere around sixty. I was helping Uncle Hubert move from his parish to the nearby cathedral of Liège. He had accepted a new assignment as one of the twelve canons who assisted the Bishop.

I was helping to load a large pick-up truck, running to and from the cellar between bombs. Some of his good friends and parishioners had loaded the baby grand piano on the truck and covered it with layers of padding. I was told to get in the cab and go with them to show the way to the new house. We were to cross over the Meuse River and go to the rue du Fer. With a piano in tow it would be a slow ride, but it could be done in less than a half hour—or so we thought.

Five minutes before departure, the sirens went off! The loud shrieking sound made our hearts skip a beat. Everyone ran for the cellar. "Whoo! This one was close," yelled our driver, rushing out to assess the damage. Before I could see anything, I heard him curse, *Les saligauds* [Filthy beasts]! and a few words that do not need to be repeated, but what we saw justified his language!

The windows of the truck were broken, the hood over the motor had disappeared, and the passenger door, attached by only one hinge, was hanging like the wing of a wounded goose. All I could think about was the beautiful piano. Though still covered, it had glass and debris piled all over it.

Using foul language I had never heard before, the driver was determined to get this load across the river. This former soldier would not let *"les Boches"* get the best of him. With heavy rope and chains, he tied the broken door to the side of the vehicle and to my seat, cleaned the glass off the seats, and threw a blanket over them. Then he turned on the ignition. The motor ran normally! He expressed his joy with another unmentionable expletive, but then the sirens sounded another alarm and back to the cellar of the rectory we ran.

If the walls of the rectory could listen, they'd have heard my uncle, along with the rest of the crew, emitting a few blasphemous words against the enemy.

They were expressing honest, human emotions in an inhumane situation, but it was comical, and I laughed hysterically all the way into and out of the cellar. Before we could make a move, the second bomb fell on Liège, but too far from us to create immediate damage.

Soon we were on our way, one energetic and determined middle-aged driver and one eighteen-year-old, holding the door by a loop of rope so that we didn't lose it.

We made it through the city and crossed the Meuse River without getting hit by several more bombs that fell too close for comfort. This former soldier had decided not to stop again for anything. We made it to the rue du Fer with half a truck and a piano "without a scratch"!

For a moment, I was elated and forgot about the bombing. The piano had arrived, and the helpers wasted no time hoisting it up to the first balcony and into the house. It rained bombs all day, but the men continued the work and finished the job. Brave men they were!

The miracle of the piano remains one of my good memories from this time.

Fernande on the rue du Fer. The baby grand piano was lifted over this balcony under a rainstorm of V1 and V2 bombs.

The Germans were retreating and the city of Liège was now overrun with American troops. They were waiting for orders to advance and defeat the enemy, to push the Germans back into Germany. The war seemed near the end. The 29th Infantry Regiment was stationed in town and remained in Liège for about four months. With the Germans out of sight and the sounds of shooting cannons now at a distance, Liège was becoming cautiously alive. While threats of bombs and enemy fire remained, people were out in the streets everywhere, greeting the liberators and be-friending them.

A strange climate blanketed the city. On the one hand, we wanted to celebrate and rejoice that liberation had finally arrived; on the other hand, the fact that the 29th was staying so long in Liège reminded us that the war was not over. Hearing cannon fire in the distance and seeing so many guards posted on the bridges crossing the Meuse River, people had ample cause for caution and concern. German spies and deserters, dressed in the uniforms of American GIs, had been reported in the city.

American soldiers were highly respected for their help and their bravery, but they were very much distrusted by my father and uncle, who had the welfare of their five daughters and nieces at heart.

At my uncle's request, my good friend Margot and I had agreed to stay together if one of us should be invited for an outing with a foreign soldier. Even at age twenty, a chaperone or companion would be desirable in their eyes.

One Sunday afternoon, Margot called to say that she had accepted a date with an American—a Private First Class named Charlie. Could I, would I, join them?

Charlie, my friend's first date, was not thrilled with my presence, and wasted no time in introducing me to his buddy, who was pulling guard at the end of the bridge that we had just crossed.

"My name is Bill," he said, keeping both hands well locked on his pointed gun. His eyes were fixed intently on everyone approaching on the bridge, obviously looking for German spies in U.S. uniforms. He looked serious and angry.

I introduced myself. At first he had difficulty pronouncing my name. He repeated it, then apologized, "I am on duty right now and can't talk, but when I am off duty, I would like to take you to the cinema."

My response was a firm "No!" During the war, if a girl had any self-respect, she did not go to the movies. Most of our Belgian young men were prisoners of war, so our prospects were mainly German soldiers. They would try to get our attention, to make a date with us. During the German occupation, the movies showed a great deal of propaganda. According to their accounts, the war was always being won by Germany! Moreover, I had never been on a serious date, and the mere thought of meeting this total stranger for one was intimidating.

I left our short encounter happy that I had given myself time to think it over, but also sorry that I lacked the courage to accept a date and take part in the fun. By now, I was so conditioned to mistrusting the unknown that dating an American soldier was not my idea of a safe activity.

A few days later, Margot called. She and Charlie had planned an outing for all four of us. We were to meet at a lovely café, a more relaxed setting where we would have a chance to get acquainted; Bill would be there.

I accepted and was pleasantly surprised to find Bill a calm and composed man who was not looking for a wild time, as Charlie was. Bill wanted to talk, and spoke of his family, whom he missed terribly. He answered many of my questions about the United States of America and told me that his Uncle Bill, for whom he was named, had been killed in Belgium in the first World War. It took no time for me to be smitten by his beautiful blue eyes, his boyish charm, and his shyness.

Liège had made a fast turnaround by opening all movie houses and showing American cinematography at its best. The four of us enjoyed a rendition of *"Sweetheart, Sweetheart, Sweetheart"* starring Jeanette MacDonald and Nelson Eddie—although Margot and I did not understand all of the English.

I felt such pride, having my first date on the arm of an American liberator. This is a wonderful memory!

Bill and I dated clandestinely for four months. Our courtship included dashing in and out of shelters to avoid buzz bombs—German V1s or V2s—when Bill would insist on covering my head with his helmet every time one of them came whistling down and destroyed half of a street.

Fernande in Bill's helmet.

My fears were justified when our short, heavenly interludes came to an abrupt end. I was lucky to have a ten-minute visit from my Bill as he rushed in to tell me that he was being shipped out. Previously, he had insisted on my getting a new hairdo and bought me a pair of white earrings. He had a photographer take my picture, to carry with him to the front lines. To his dismay, however, the picture was not ready, and I had to send it to him a few days later.

The Belgian people had been telling the Americans that they were becoming complacent about the dangers of this war. For us the war was far from over, but the guys would make fun of our fears and try to calm our nerves. "Have another glass of wine and relax," they would say. Relax!! I think we all learned that casual word. It helped with our paranoia.

The photo of Fernande that Bill took with him to the front.

On December 16, 1944, the Battle of the Bulge erupted; this was the last major German counter-offensive of World War II. Hitler wanted to push the Allies, who had reached Bastogne, back up through Belgium and to Paris.

The city of Liège was divided by the Meuse River. Those of us who lived on the south side of the river were ordered to cross over to the north side of the city. All bridges

over the Meuse would be blown up again, this time by the Germans, to stop Allied reinforcements from coming down to Bastogne from the north.

People made a dash for the bridges to get to the other side of the river. Another evacuation! But this time, there was no time to pack anything. The object was to get across the river before the returning enemy could stop us.

Uncle Hubert was already at the cathedral on the north side. He called and told me to leave immediately and to leave everything behind. The Germans had already started to bomb Liège, and the fear of their return created panic in the city.

I ran to the closest wooden bridge. I was almost across when I heard the dreaded whistling sound of a V-bomb coming down. I sprinted, trying to make it to the other side, afraid the bomb would hit the *passerelle*, as we called all pedestrian bridges. The sound of the descending bomb had now become a verdict of death. Yes, it fell, smack in the middle of my *passerelle*.

The blast of the bomb must have propelled my body to the end of the bridge. There I was, flat on my stomach, caught over the crack where the bridge had split. Half of my body struggled to hold on to a piece of railing that I had grabbed; the other half gravitated toward the water. I thought this would surely be my end. Struggling with my other hand to grab another piece of wood did not help lift me to the top where I thought I could crawl to safety. For a brief moment, panic struck. I thought of giving up.

Maybe I should let go and try to swim toward the embankment, I considered. Suddenly, a strong hand grabbed my wrist and, with the help of another, pulled my body over the edge, from the tilted plank of wood to safety.

Looking up from the stretcher they had forced me onto, I saw two angels. They had great faces, heads covered with helmets, and spoke a language that I barely understood. They were bending over me to see if I was going to make it. Americans, of course! Medics or bridge guards? I'll never know, but to me they were the bravest of the brave, who had saved my life. I found out later that around sixty people had drowned.

Many men died before Hitler's defeat. The war was not over. Bombs kept falling, inflicting many more trials and tribulations on the people of Liège, Belgium, and throughout Europe.

I spent many nights standing on the balcony of my bedroom in prayers and in tears, listening to the rumblings of battle and imagining my Bill in harm's way. On his departure, he gave me this order: "You will look at the moon every night, send love and kisses, and remember that someday we shall be together." It was our mutual vow, our secret engagement!

Little did we know then that those dreams and promises would not come true for five more years.

My life had changed so drastically. I was in love and living on hope, and Bill and I had a moonlight rendezvous every night.

Fernande and Bill in the park in Liège, Belgium—1945.

Lonely and with no place to go, I stayed in Liège and worked for Uncle Hubert until the end of the war. My favorite activity became the daily trip to the mail box, always hoping for a letter from the front.

U.S. mail was light and slow, but after a few letters had arrived, the one that broke my heart made its way to Uncle's mailbox. It announced Bill's repatriation to the States.

Bill was wounded! A piece of shrapnel coming from a nearby mine explosion had hit his head. His letter said that he was in a military hospital and would be going back to the States shortly.

"Never forget our moonlight rendezvous," he wrote, "You will hear from me, and we shall be together soon."

My family was still under great stress. The house where they lived after the bombing of our home in Montzen was too small for everyone. Also, for the second time in his life, Dad had been robbed of his livelihood, of his way of caring for the family. In World War I and again in World War II, his business had been destroyed.

There was little or no money, and food was scarce. The Belgian government had instituted a new law whereby restitution for war damage could be received only when proprietors could match the gift. Our homestead was not restored for another six years.

There was but one solution for survival. Brothers and sisters who were old enough banded together and found jobs in the cities or anywhere they were available. We all worked to sustain the family.

On weekends, Uncle would pay my train fare, and I'd go back and forth between Liège and home. If someone needed help during the weekend in Montzen, I would work to bring extra food or money. I remember one weekend job when a farmer needed someone to pick potatoes behind the plow. I offered to work with the hope of bringing home a bucket of potatoes for my family. The farmer paid me for my backbreaking day's work with a big ham sandwich—not even a meal for the family. I was disappointed and insulted at my meager pay. I carried my sandwich home to share with my younger siblings.

Papa, (who was on total disability as a result of World War I) worked all day in the garden and supplied fruit and vegetables for the table. Brother Hubert used to see Papa hiding in the garden after a meager meal. He would pick raw vegetables like cabbage leaves and lettuce to chew on so as not to let mother know that he was still hungry.

Every Saturday, all working children would report home with their earnings. Maman would give us a little allowance to go back to our jobs and a few francs for a small bar of chocolate. I used to enjoy going home on weekends when Maman would make a chocolate pudding or special waffles for Sunday's dessert.

She would wait for the time when her children were home, gather the family together and say, "Now come, and let's talk about your week." She always wanted to know if we had done a good job and what had made us happy during that time away from home.

After much conversation, Papa would start our traditional family sing-along. He firmly believed that everyone had a voice, so abstention was not an option. He loved hearing Maman's beautiful soprano voice, while he held his own with his strong, deep bass. Hubert would grab his flute, and for an hour or so, we would sing our whole repertoire of songs: family favorites, religious songs of prayer, even popular bar songs from the *carnaval* of Coln. People passing by would stop and listen to our family chorus. These were such loving interludes that they made us forget the suffering that the war had dealt us.

The first song that would be intoned by Dad, and that remains a tradition when we get together today, is the simple song *Où peut-on être mieux qu'au sein de sa famille,* which posed the timeless question, "Where could one be happier than in the bosom of one's family?" This song embodied our feelings and happiness at being gathered together again.

On April 28, 1946, disaster struck our family like never before. Maman died in my arms of a sudden coronary occlusion. I can still cry when I remember Papa and all eight children gathered around her grave! The stress and silent pain of war had claimed her life.

I thought of Bill and our prospective future. How could I possibly approach the subject of leaving the family anytime soon?

There would be three more years of moonlight rendezvous before my dreams of life with Bill would come to pass.

* * * * *

By 1947, we had struggled for almost a year to create a life without Maman. Since her death, my oldest sister Bertha had taken charge of the household. Cecile, our youngest sibling, had been confirmed, and Papa was able to take advantage of help from the state and the family.

Letters from Bill had inexplicably dwindled to zero. *Had he decided that for me to leave my family would be too painful?* For whatever reason, there were no letters. This treatment left me perplexed. I could not write to him with reproach or force him into a commitment that might make him feel uncomfortable. *Could he have made a promise he could not keep?*

For me, the decision was made. It was Bill or no one else! After two years of waiting to hear from him, I decided to return to school and find a useful niche in the world. Many hours of private tutoring helped me to pass a state entrance exam and gain acceptance to Brussels University School of Nursing, where I successfully completed my second year. I was ready to forget about the idea of marriage and make nursing a career.

Four years had passed without knowledge of Bill. One day, while on lunch break, I wandered into the mailroom of our nurses' center and let out a scream of joy. In my mail slot was a letter, bordered in red, white and blue stripes! "Bill!" I screamed, running up the stairs to my room to fetch my *Assimil*, a book of French/English translation. This left the rest of the class stunned and dying of curiosity.

"What has happened to Catgut (a nickname I had earned)? they asked.

Against regulation, I stayed in my room to decipher the delicious words in this letter. No, he had not forgotten about me, but wanted to know why I never answered his letters. "Did you change your mind?" he asked. "Are you married, and are you happy? I need to have an answer. Please respond."

Bill had sent his "last letter" to Margot, asking her to get it to me. She knew that I was in Brussels in school, and kindly followed Bill's request.

With too much time lost already, I sent an immediate response, which read, "No, I didn't receive your letters! No, I'm not married! No, I'm not happy!" I signed it, "Love, Perplexed." I received a stiff demerit for not showing up at the lunch table with our professor that day.

Bill's answer came swiftly and without reproach. He just assumed that after my long silence something had gone wrong. The only question he asked this time was, "Will you please marry me now?"

My answer was equally swift: "Yes! Yes! Yes!" I'd search for an explanation later. This was not a rash decision. My heart spoke it without the help of my brain. My decision never changed; it was locked away there forever.

The dilemma that I would face with my loving family would be far greater than anything I had experienced during the entire war. How could I approach Papa, who had suffered so much loss in his life? How would I get his blessing to leave my family, my country, and the rewards of all my hard work? I thought of only one person: Uncle Hubert! He would give me advice. He would know how to handle the situation.

I went to Liège the first Sunday that I was free and announced Bill's news to my dear uncle. He stood there in shock, then walked three circles around his big desk. With tears in his eyes, he told me to go home and inform my father of this "sad" event.

Papa was speechless as he listened intently to me. My brothers and sisters were astonished. They stood frozen *sur place* [without moving] in disbelief, unable to grasp the gravity of the moment.

I spent the night talking to my sister Mary. She confided in me that, against Papa's instructions, yes, letters from Bill had arrived and had been confiscated by my father. He told her that he had promised Maman during the war that if anything should happen to her, he would personally watch over her children. If I went to America, he felt that he could never keep that promise. Mary was sworn to secrecy and, while she disagreed strongly with Papa, she felt guilty breaking her promise to him.

I promised Mary that Papa would never find out from me that I knew this secret. I could see my poor heartsick Dad, with eight children to worry about, making life and death decisions for his five girls, especially a rebel like me, not knowing the right thing to do. He would often tell his sister, Aunt Bella, my godmother, that he was overwhelmed with these girls, that he didn't know how to manage their social lives.

I could just picture him, carefully putting Bill's unopened letters in his left inside pocket, where he put all important papers, and saying to himself, *I will have to think about this, sleep on it.* When I learned what my father had done to stop this marriage, a love/hate relationship surfaced for a while, but I could never condemn his actions.

He should not be rejected for doing what he believed was right, I thought. I forgave him and kept my promise to Mary. It was enough for me to know that Bill had told the truth. He had written, and knowing that reinforced the deep trust I had in him.

When I returned to college the next day, there was a message from the Head Mistress of Nursing. She told me that I was allotted three days of relief from classes to attend counseling sessions with my uncle's best friend, Father Hanotte, a priest/psychiatrist. I was to attend mass in the morning and two counseling sessions, one in the morning and one in the afternoon, each of the three days. Uncle Hubert had called the directress of the school to set up this program to help me make the right decision.

I look back at those three days as a time of deep reflection, prayer, and eventually peace. I thank God for the fatherly help and prayers that my dear uncle and Father Hanotte bestowed on me. In the final analysis, I found my answer and my strength.

I went to my last counseling session with apprehension but, to my amazement, Father Hanotte approved of my marriage to Bill and gave me his blessing. "You must go to Bill," he said. "It is your destiny."

A plane ticket arrived in my mailbox three months later—a one-way trip to the United States!! For the moment, it was sheer ecstasy, although I knew that the next few weeks would be bittersweet.

My joy was tainted by the powerful odds stacked against me for leaving the family. There was my oldest sister Bertha and my oldest brother Joseph, who were angry at my "adventure," as they called it. Dear Mary, my closest sister, was sure that if I left for the USA, she would never see me again. The most heart-wrenching obstacle to overcome, however, would be Papa.

I was determined not to leave without my father's blessing. Arriving home on a one-day leave, I told Papa that I needed to talk to him. He picked up his Panama hat and cane and invited me to the garden.

Papa always discussed important things in the garden. Together, we had once built a gazebo with table and benches which was now enclosed by beautiful lilac trees and rose bushes, for privacy reasons.

"Papa," I said, "Bill has sent me a proposal of marriage and an airline ticket to go to the United States. He promised that we will return for a visit to the family as soon as possible."

There was a moment of silence. Then, in a soft gentle voice, he went into all the reasons for his disapproval of my marrying Bill, and insisted that I forget this whole episode of my life.

"I have promised your mother to take care of you. How can I do that with you so far away?"

We argued for the longest time, while I pointed out that I was twenty-four, and old enough to take care of myself. Most of all, I assured him that I was in love with Bill.

Then came the harshest warning from my kind but stern father. "You do know," he said, "that if you take this step, Fernande, there will be no coming back. Marriage is a serious commitment, both to man and to God. If it is a mistake, you will have to live with it. You will not be able to come back home to live with us."

Exhausted from the passionate discussion, we walked back to the kitchen to have a hot cup of coffee. Papa realized that I was as determined then as when I had refused to work for the Germans.

He needed silence to think it over. A heartbreaking silence it was. Papa looked sad and defeated. I felt guilty for putting him through such pain and anguish.

By then I had decided that I could not and would not leave my family without his blessing. I wanted to end the arguments. After a quiet moment and a silent prayer, I pulled my airline ticket out of my pocket and softly slid it on the table in front of him saying, "Papa, here is my plane ticket. I cannot marry Bill without your approval. If you cannot give me your blessing, then please, YOU tear up the ticket, because I can't."

With tears rolling down his beautiful white beard, he put his hand on top of mine, slid the ticket back to me, and said: "Now you know, Kinneque, (his pet Dutch dialect word meaning "little one") that I could not do that. That would mean that I was running your life for you. I would not and could not do that!" We both cried, fell into each other's arms, and embraced! Suddenly, after the long dark night, I saw sunlight on the horizon.

Times and circumstances had changed indeed! After all we'd gone through—occupation, evacuation, separation, life in hiding, bombing, loss of home and business, death of Maman—we no longer needed to sleep with one eye open. We felt safe again in the bosom of our family, and hopeful about the future. Life with Bill would be the cheerful exclamation point on that chapter of my life.

Wedding photograph. Fernande and Bill—October 27, 1949.

Epilogue

I did not return to that *safe haven* until seven years later, when Bill and I decided to take a trip to Belgium. We wanted to be with the family to celebrate my brother Hubert's ordination to the priesthood. The train took us from Brussels to Herbestal, where we expected one of my brothers or sisters to be waiting to take us back to Montzen. Our beautiful European express was now slowly rolling into the station, when suddenly Bill joyfully exclaimed, "There's Papa!" proud that he saw him first. This was extraordinary, because he had never met Papa! Sure enough, there he was, standing alone on the platform: Panama hat, bow tie, his beautiful white beard, and his cane. He had come in person, had hired a taxi to take us back to Montzen, and gave us a glorious welcome home. The best cigars and the best liqueurs were offered as we were wined and dined.

Papa at age 83.

One day when the family was seated together in the living room, Papa was staring at Bill with admiration and listening to his English conversation with my brother. Papa could not understand much of what they were discussing, but he turned to me and said, "Yes, my dear, I was wrong about Bill. You have a fine gentleman for a husband, and I have a great son-in-law!"

Bill had become the family's hero! One of the liberators of our land!

I thanked Papa for his welcome and for loving Bill. I was happy to know that he had made his peace with my decision.

* * * * *

Back home in the States, not long ago, I was asked by someone how I felt about the liberators who had done so much damage and inflicted so much pain on our hometown people. The question was an overwhelming one, and I didn't really know how to answer it. I hated war, not the people who were made to fight it.

From childhood, we were taught in school that Germans were our enemies. People hated them for the atrocities they had committed in World War I and for the devastation they left behind in Belgium in 1918. Teachers had nothing good to say about the people or the country. Gestapo, Wehrmacht, Boches, Nazi—Germans were to be feared and hated. However, we were told to learn German in case the enemy returned to our land; we would need to be able to defend ourselves! "We must remember," said our teacher, "we live only a few kilometers from Aachen!" On a good day we could almost see the forest of Aachen, Germany, from our bedroom windows, but no one ever traveled there! I crossed that dreaded border for the first time in 1956, with my American husband, on our way to Switzerland.

I know we were supposed to hate the Germans, but over the years, when faced with German people, I could not hate anybody. It never entered my mind. On the contrary, I was curious about them, and wanted to know more about them and what life was like on the other side of that border.

In wartime, I must admit that if someone was standing in front of me, pointing a gun at me, ready to terminate my life by simply pulling the trigger, self-defense would take over. It would have nothing to do with hate; it would be survival. Or, when I recovered from the shock of a German bomb exploding close by, surrounded by death and destruction, I felt only hate for those who were the cause of these crimes. I don't even know if I wanted revenge; I just wanted to get them out of our country, out of our sight.

But there were times when feelings blurred.

I recall at the beginning of the war, while Mademoiselle and I were back in Andenne after our evacuation and on an errand through the countryside, the arm of a dead soldier was found and properly buried by the authorities of the village. I was terribly shocked by the incident and set out to look for the rest of the person's body. Though I never found it, I was profoundly sad. It did not matter whether the dead man was German or Belgian. I was just sick at heart for this poor soul and wanted to find his remains, to bury him with dignity.

Soon after this, I was sent to fetch milk from the farm of Madeleine's friend. I decided to drag my bicycle and take a shortcut through the lush green meadow flanking the long road to the farm. As I approached a huge oak tree that dominated the beautiful meadow, I saw a soldier lying on the ground at the base of the tree. I recognized the German helmet hanging over the butt of his rifle, which was planted upside down in the ground. This was the customary way for the military to indicate that a soldier was dead.

I threw my bike on the grass and carefully approached him. This was in 1940, and my first experience with a fallen enemy at close range! A German, lying there, incapable of shooting me! I had seen so many people machine-gunned during our evacuation. I was happy that he was not "one of ours." He was German alright, and he was dead. He could no longer harm me.

His hand was folded over his chest as if he had been reaching for the small upper pocket of his uniform. I saw two small pictures pulled halfway out of the pocket and, for a brief moment, thought I saw him move to reach them. A figment of my imagination! I didn't know what to do. I wasn't sure that I should even touch him.

I knelt down next to him, reached over and pulled the pictures all the way out of his pocket. Two small beautiful children—his, no doubt. Sick at heart, I replaced them and told this good-looking blond father, in German, how sorry I was for him and for his children. I spoke to him as though he were alive. Then, still kneeling over his body, I prayed the "Our Father" for him, again in German, and burst into tears. I left hurriedly, for fear someone would see me and call me a traitor. I was heartbroken, but never told a soul about my experience or my conflicted heart. There was no room for hate! Only sadness!

As for the Allies who bombed Montzen, they were heaven-sent liberators of our country and victims, like us, of a madman's tyranny. Those young men came to Belgium from so far away to rescue us, to save people they had never known or seen. They saved so many of us and returned thousands of prisoners of war to their families. They gave us back our liberty.

My feelings were, and still are, that I owe the Americans an immense debt of gratitude. To me they were the bravest men on earth.

May the Lord bless them all.

* * * * *

Discussion Questions

General

1. What was the role of faith in Fernande's mission and survival?

2. How did Papa's advice to Fernande influence her actions during the war?

3. What personal qualities inspired her to take the risks she did as a member of the Resistance?

4. Why was Uncle Hubert's role in the war a great inspiration to Fernande?

5. How did Fernande's command of German help her?

6. In general, how did the Belgian people demonstrate their resistance to the German occupiers?

7. What role did hate play in the events of the era?

8. Can breaking the law ever be justified? If so, under what circumstances?

9. In Fernande's place, what would you have done when you learned that Bill had been sending letters?

10. What was the German reaction as the end of the war neared?

11. What lessons can be learned from Fernande's experiences in the war?

Content-Directed

1. Describe the family's village life before the war.

2. Why was the viaduct significant? How did it change the small town of Montzen Gare?

3. Why was May 10, 1940 a "fateful day"?

4. How did the people's memories of the first World War influence their reactions to German invasion?

5. Describe/illustrate the exodus of families on the road south, to presumed safety in France.

6. Describe the situation in the makeshift bunker on the farm.

7. Why was Fernande asked to work for the Germans? In what capacity? What was her reaction?

8. Why were cows lying upside down in the fields?

9. Describe the villa, upon Fernande's and Mademoiselle's return to Andenne.

10. Why did Fernande return home on foot? List examples of what she then finds, to illustrate her statement that "nothing was the same"?

11. Why was sock mending significant?

12. How was being annexed different from being occupied?

13. How did school life change after annexation? Why?

14. How were people forced to help the German war effort?

15. How did Uncle Alphonse and Aunt Martine help the Resistance?

16. What did people do to avoid starvation?

17. Why did Fernande take the risk of asking to see the Commandant?

18. Why were young people drafted by the German government?

19. According to the draft papers, what would happen if Fernande did not report to the train that would take her to her work assignment in an ammunition factory?

20. When Fernande left for the train, Papa gave her some advice. Describe how it affected her later behavior.

21. Why was secrecy so important among all members of the underground? Why could no one be trusted?

22. Give examples of Uncle Hubert's activities during the war. What did those in hiding in the Rectory do when German soldiers rang the doorbell in the middle of the night?

23. Why was Fernande especially valuable in her underground missions?

24. Why was it important to know one's false identity by heart?

25. How did the actions of Josh/Pierre put himself and the Resistance in danger?

26. How and why did the Germans block off traffic in and out of a city square?

27. How did Fernande save herself and the young boy on the road to Banneux?

28. Why did the Germans release the clergy from prison? Why did Uncle Hubert ignore Fernande at that time?

29. Why was the railway station in Montzen increasingly important to the war effort?

30. How did Papa and Joseph assure the safety of the family during the bombing?

31. Describe the attack on Montzen Gare and its aftermath.

32. Give some examples of sabotage. Why had it become a way of life for children and adults?

33. Why was it important to help fallen airmen?

34. What was the Rexist movement? Why was it dangerous?

35. Describe the Belgian people's reaction on the arrival of the American troops.

36. Which of Fernande's acts of daring most impressed you? Why?

37. Why did Fernande insist on returning home despite the fighting still raging on the border?

38. Why did Bill and Fernande date in secret? What was their mutual vow when he was shipped out?

39. Life after liberation: How did the family survive without business to support them?

40. Explain the tradition of singing in the family. Why was that important?

41. Why did letters from Bill stop arriving?

42. Why did Papa refuse to let Fernande marry Bill?

43. Did Fernande condemn his action? Why not?

44. Why was life in Liège so dangerous after the arrival of the U.S. troops?

45. Explain the meaning of the subtitle, *A Wakeful Eye in the Underground*. Refer specifically to the definition of "wakeful" and what Fernande writes in that regard.

Question base by Emily Z. Wagner & Donna J. Merow

Fernande Davis in her trademark blue hat, dedicating a copy of her book, after receiving a standing ovation for speaking at the American Association of Teachers of French conference in Liège, Belgium (July 2008). (photo Emily Z. Wagner)

REFERENCES USED

Jackson, Julian. *The Fall of France: The Nazi Invasion of 1940.* New York: Oxford University Press, 2003. (Photograph, bottom p. 175).

Uncredited booklet *Montzen-Gare se souvient [Montzen-Gare remembers]* ! Belgium, ca. 1985. (Photographs, pp. 9, 10 bottom, 11 bottom, 12 upper right.)

Interviews with Mr. and Mrs. Vercheval, of Jahay, Belgium, and with Mr. and Mrs. Jean-Pierre Gillot of Seilles (formerly Seilles/Andenne).

FURTHER STUDY

BIBLIOGRAPHY

Burgett, Donald R. *Seven Roads to Hell: A Screaming Eagle at Bastogne.* New York: Bantam Dell Books, 2000.

Demoulin, Germaine. *Le Journal de Germaine Demoulin: Montzen 18.01.1941–15.09.1944. Chronique d'une famille de passeurs.* Helios et Obelit. Document d'histoire I-Montzen 2006.

Diamond, Hanna. *Fleeing Hitler: France 1940.* London: Oxford University Press, 2007.

Eisner, Peter. *The Freedom Line: The Brave Men and Women Who Rescued Allied Airmen from the Nazis During World War II.* New York: Perenniel, 2005.

Eman, Diet with James Schaap. *Things We Couldn't Say.* Grand Rapids: Wm. B. Eerdmans, 1999.

Michman, Dan (editor). A volume of essays, *Belgium and the Holocaust: Jews, Belgians, Germans.* Published by Yad Vashem in 1998 and in 2000.

Schrijvers, Peter. *The Unknown Dead: Civilians in the Battle of the Bulge.* University Press of Kentucky, 2005.

Vroman, Suzanne. *Hidden Children of the Holocaust: Belgian Nuns and Their Daring Rescue of Jewish Youths from the Nazis.* New York: Oxford University Press, 2008.

VIDEOGRAPHY

Last Best Hope: A True Story of Escape, Evasion and Remembrance. DVD. PBS, 2006.

Petit Garcon. Dir. by Pierre Granier-Deferre. Perf. Jacques Weber, Brigitte Roüan, Stanislas Crevillen, Ludmila Mikael. TF1 Film Production/ Canal+,1995.

As If It Were Yesterday (Comme si c'était hier). Dir. by Myriam Abramowicz and Esther Hoffenberg. Written by National Center for Jewish Film. Documentary in French with English subtitles, 1980.

WEBOGRAPHY (verified February 2008)

WHKMLA: History of Belgium, 1940–1945. World War II timeline, details on Belgium of the early 1940's.
www.zum.de/whkmla/region/lowcountries/bel194045.html

Resistance Movements: The Resistance movements in Europe during World War II played an important part in defeating Nazi Germany's military might.
www.historylearningsite.co.uk/resistance_movements.htm

The History Net/World War II/Tiny Mulder: Teenage World War II Resistance Heroine.
www.historynet.com/wars_conflicts/world_war_2/3023766.html

WWII – Europe – Resistance – Others
(included under Belgium) Bodson, Herman. *Agent for the Resistance: A Belgian Saboteur in World War II.* College Station, TX: Texas A & M University Press, 1994.

intellit.org/wwii_folder/wwiieurope_folder/wwiieurresother.html

Ouvrages disponibles chez
Beach Lloyd Publishers, LLC

Darkness Hides the Flowers : A True Story of Holocaust Survival
— Jerry L. Jennings, as told by Ida Hoffmann Firestone

Sarah's Key — Tatiana de Rosnay
Elle s'appelait Sarah — T. de Rosnay (French edition)

Drôle de Mémoires en Normandie — Armand Idrac
Avant-propos d'Emmanuel Le Roy Ladurie
Memoirs from Normandy: Childhood, War & Life's Adventures
— Armand Idrac, traduit et relu par Joanne S. Silver

*Ma Normandie à Moi : Un jeune homme vit la Deuxième Guerre
mondiale* — A. Idrac ; avant-propos d'Emmanuel Le
Roy Ladurie, rédigé par J. S. Silver
My Normandy: A Teenager lives through World War II —
A. Idrac ; traduit, relu et compilé par J. S. Silver

Visages de la Shoah : Marcel Jabelot — Barbara P. Barnett
Faces of the Holocaust : Marcel Jabelot
VHS / DVD en français, option de sous-titres en anglais
Faces of the Holocaust : Marcel Jabelot (livre) —
B. P. Barnett

*Tu t'appelles Renée : Paroles d'une Enfant Cachée dans la
France de Vichy (1940–1944)*
Traduit par Ruth Kapp Hartz dont c'est l'histoire
Avant-propos de Beate Klarsfeld — Stacy Cretzmeyer
Guide d'Étude pour le livre Tu t'appelles Renée by Stacy
Cretzmeyer — J. Silver

*Your Name is Renée: Ruth Kapp Hartz's Story as a Hidden
Child in Vichy France* — Stacy Cretzmeyer
Avant-propos de Beate Klarsfeld
DVD *Voices of Holocaust History: Ruth Tells Her Story* —
Deanne Scherlis Comer
Study Guide for the book Your Name is Renée by Stacy
Cretzmeyer — J. S. Silver

141

La France dans la Seconde Guerre mondiale — Gérard Vial

Un costume rayé d'enfer — Jean-Pierre Renouard

Au Revoir les enfants (texte, activités) — Louis Malle
    présenté par L. Parodi et M. Vallacco (texte, activités)
DVD *Au Revoir les enfants* 101 mins., choice of English subtitles
    — L. Malle

*Mon Enfance lilloise racontée à ma fille : Récits d'antan
    (1950 à 1955)* — Denis Herbert
Complément Éducatif : Mon Enfance lilloise racontée à ma fille
    — D. Herbert & J. S. Silver

La filière des enfants — Jean-François Elberg

*War Orphan in San Francisco: Letters Link a Family Scattered by
    World War II* (2nd edition) — Phyllis Helene Mattson

*French Philadelphia: The French Cultural & Historical Presence
    in the Delaware Valley —*
    Lynn H. Miller & Annette H. Emgarth
    Photography, Emmanuel Pierre Gee
*Philadelphie à la française : la présence culturelle et
    historique des Français dans la vallée de la Delaware —*
    L. H. Miller et A. H. Emgarth, photographies par E. P. Gee

Musique : *Les Chansons sous l'Occupation : French Songs
    of WWII,* Arkadia Entertainment Corp., New York
Complement to the CD Les Chansons sous l'Occupation —
    J. S. Silver

DVD *Voices of Holocaust History : A Curriculum Project*
DVD *Voices of Holocaust History : Eva Tells Her Story*
DVD *Voices of Holocaust History : Liesl Tells Her Story*
                    — Deanne Scherlis Comer

Suite française (Némirovsky), English edition

Contact Beach Lloyd Publishers for recent imports.

Beach Lloyd
PUBLISHERS
LLC

Web: http://www.BEACHLLOYD.com
E-mail: BEACHLLOYD@erols.com
Phone: (610) 407-9107 or
Cell: (215) 407-4570
Fax: (775) 254-0633

40 Cabot Drive
Wayne, PA 19087-5619

QUICK Order Form

⌸ **Fax orders**: 775-254-0633. Send this form.

☎ **Telephone orders**: Call 610-407-9107 or
cell phone 215-407-4570

💻 **E-mail orders**: BEACHLLOYD@erols.com

🖅 **Postal Orders**: Beach Lloyd Publishers, LLC
Joanne S. Silver, Mgr.
40 Cabot Drive
Wayne, PA 19087-5619
USA

Please send the following books & other products:

_____

_____

_____

Name: _____

Address: _____

City: _____ State: _____ ZIP: _____

Telephone: _____

E-mail address: _____

Sales tax: Please add 6% for products shipped to Pennsylvania addresses.

Shipping: **U.S.**: approximately $6 for 1-3 books.

International: approximately $12; contact for estimate.

Payment: Check or Money Order in US dollars, payable to
Beach Lloyd Publishers, LLC.

Visit www.BEACHLLOYD.com for more information on products and pricing, as well as presentations to schools and groups.